for ye violls

The consort and dance music
of William Lawes

David Pinto

Fretwork
1995

Fretwork Editions, 67 Kings Road, Richmond, Surrey TW10 6EG
General Editors: Bill Hunt & Julia Hodgson

ISBN 1–898131–04–X

Printed in Great Britain

Cover reproduction of an anonymous portrait, believed to be of William Lawes, by kind permission of the Faculty of Music, Oxford University.

Contents

Abbreviations

Periodicals and music series

AM	*Acta Musicologica*
CMM	*Corpus Mensurabilis Musicæ*
ECS	*English Consort Series*
ELS	*The English Lute-Songs*
EM	*Early Music*
EMR	*Early Music Review*
EMS	*The English Madrigal School*
GSJ	*Journal of the Galpin Society*
Grove 5	*Grove's Dictionary of Music and Musicians 5th edn (1954–61)*
Grove 6	*Grove's Dictionary 6th edn = The New Grove (1980)*
JEFDSS	*Journal of the English Folk Dance and Song Society*
JRMA	*see PRMA*
JVdGSA	*Journal of the Viola da Gamba Society of America*
LSJ	*The Lute Society Journal*
M&L	*Music & Letters*
MA	*The Musical Antiquary*
MB	*Musica Britannica*
MD	*Musica Disciplina*
MQ	*The Musical Quarterly*
P(R)MA	*Proceedings of the (Royal) Musical Association; subsequently Journal*
RECM	*Records of English Court Music*
RMA	*The Royal Musical Association*
RRMBE	*Recent Researches in the Music of the Baroque Era*
RRMR	*Recent Researches in the Music of the Renaissance*
SP	*Supplementary Publication(s) (Viola da Gamba Society)*

F/	facsimile
R/	reprint
2/	2nd edition

Library Sigla

Great Britain
GB-Ckc   Cambridge, King's College Library
GB-DRc   Durham Cathedral, Dean and Chapter Library
GB-Lbl   London, British Library
GB-Lcm   London, Royal College of Music;
GB-Lms   London, Madrigal Society collection
GB-Ob   Oxford, Bodleian Library
GB-Och   Oxford, Christ Church
GB-T   Tenbury, St Michael's College

France
F-Pc   Paris, Conservatoire MSS (in Paris, Bibliothèque Nationale)
F-Pn   Paris, Bibliothèque Nationale

United States of America
US-NH   Yale University at New Haven
US-NYp   New York, Public Library
US-SM   San Marino

Subscribers

The publishers are grateful to the following for their
support in the publication of this book

Anne Appleton
Quentin Appleton
Andrew Ashbee
Derry Bertenshaw
C. Blacker
Richard Bodig
Richard Boothby
John Bryan
Richard Campbell
John Catch
Richard Charteris
Paul Cheshire
Christopher Coggill
Christophe Coin
John Cousen
Alison Crum
Sarah Cunningham
Paul Denley
John Drackley
Laurence Dreyfus
Catherine Finnis
Michael Fleming
Pierre Funck
Wendy Gillespie
Clare Griffel
Marjorie Harmer
Linda Hill

Michael Hobbs
Gill Humphrys
Anne Keynes
Jeremy Kinglake-Jones
Michèle Kohler
Wieland Kuijken
Heather Ling
Richard Luckett
Gerhard Lutz
Jeremy Maule
Rita Morey
Chester Pearlman
Susanna Pell
Lucy Robinson
Tristram Robson
Anthony Rowland-Jones
Kazuya Sato
Roger Spikes
Julie Stobbs
Les Stobbs
Peter Syrus
Jochen Thesmann
D. Tibet
Anthony van Kampen
José Vasquez
Robin Woodbridge
Daniel Yeadon

Prelude

Sunday, 21st March, 1641. The atmosphere in the street had been uneasy, a combination of the cold but close prevailing weather and the menacing aspect of the gaggles of armed young mohocks (king's men, they would term themselves!) clustering round the hackney. It is a relief to be off the street. Your letters give access to a long, dark-panelled corridor, from which one glances back to the bright wall of the Privy Garden on the south side of Whitehall. There are further turnings ahead, leading to the commoners' entrance to the Cockpit-in-Court, which is fanned by a welcome breeze off Saint James' Park. The grooms outside are prominently girt with rapiers, however unlikely it is that the king will attend, owing to extraordinary privy council meetings: the times are troubled, as is only too tempting to put from the mind. He is probably composing his mind for the weighty affair of the morrow when all the world will repair to Westminster Hall and inaugurate the tribunal for committal proceedings in the cause célèbre, *the arraignment of his trusted minister, the hated Earl of Strafford. The full hearing begins on Tuesday. Few public trials have been so momentous since that of the Earl of Essex, forty years ago in old Elizabeth's day. Just as well, since you would not have felt easy in the shadow of Charles Stuart at the moment. Your position as Clerk to the House of Lords makes you over-conspicuous in the coming legal affray, now that your father-in-law Packer, a man of principle, has incurred the stigma of ingratitude for refusing the king a forced loan; they had thought him pliable enough up to now. Still, without that office, one of the rare tickets giving entry to the royal theatre would have been less readily granted by the Master of Ceremonies. Not that you have ever petitioned to watch the usual cavalier posturings; the lewd stagings in playhouses, the cavortings held in the queen's 'dancing barn' along the street, let alone the absurdly overblown and costly masques like the recent scurrilous* Salmacida Spolia. *Fantasy music, though, is a different brew of ale, especially when new music is on tap. Within, you recognise faces in the* mêlée: *drawn like you to hear what Master Lawes has up his sleeve. The 'Presence' has been lowered to its place in the centre of the auditorium. In default of the king, his nephew may take his place there; for Charles Louis, the Elector Palatine, has made an unheralded visit to*

1

court last week. Now a knot of courtiers emerges out of the king's side. Endymion Porter's familiar face looms out: a cultured gentleman of the bedchamber, recently grown high in favour. Who is his equally rubicund attendant? He wears an unkempt minister's dress, but is no chaplain; and nothing about his roving eye damps your apprehension as he sizes up your young wife Elizabeth. You are torn between exasperation and amusement as he scrapes acquaintance by proffering her a couple of flowery compliments. Agreeably surprised by his enthusiasm for varying forms of music, you gather that he is an old friend of Nicholas Lanier, Master of the Music, and has provided verse for court occasions in past years. It is not surprising then that you had not met, since modern vocal music has for you few charms compared to the old style you grew up with in your uncle's house; the sacred part-songs and string-accompanied verse anthems—all now unfashionable, alas! Happily your reverend acquaintance Herrick agrees with you over the uplifting force of the older music; as he himself terms it, 'dead things with inbreath'd sense able to pierce'—not his own term, but that of a scrivener's son, he explains with an odd sideways mow. He knows Henry Lawes too, and has rubbed shoulders with William; though that in itself does not make his manners any the less suspect. The handwritten bill by the doors had listed the other entertainment: recitative and songs with continued bass. But if the spirit does not inform them and they are out of keeping with the Sabbath recreation, they cannot enthral, for howsoever many voices they are written. Spare thought for the surroundings: one dines out on such details.

The great branches of the candelabra are now being lighted, though subdued day from the lantern twenty-eight feet above had sufficed to take in the layout of the seats. They are disposed on five sides of the twenty-foot octagon: all banked, but skewed so as not to turn disrespectful backs on the Presence. A star-spangled blue calico cloth has been drawn aside from the skylights on gleaming copper rings. On the rear wall behind the assembly are illumined two great pieces of painted work: a David and Goliath, and Saul's Conversion on the road to Damascus—by Parma, you gather. Also mounted alongside them can be seen the Twelve Cæsars, work of the great Titian. The stage-front to which heads now turn raises a classical proscenium, two storeys high and thirty feet across. Its lower order has five doorways, the central one flanked by pedestals carrying plaster-of-Paris statues named Melpomene and Thalia. In the upper, the niches are filled

2

with statue busts of Sophocles, Euripides, Aeschylus and Aristophanes. There is a curved pediment, bearing a tablet inscribed 'Prodesse & Delectare' beneath two recumbent genii; above that are two busts on brackets, the fathers of tragedy and comedy, Thespis and Epicharmus. The king's Surveyor-General Inigo Jones took his inspiration from the Teatro Olimpico at Vicenza, your new clergyman friend murmurs as he points out all the restrained beauties of this blue and gold luxury. One thing sits oddly: a chamber organ placed before the façade.

Some of the livery-clad musical servants walk through to backstage, among them Will Lawes. You get the merest of acknowledgements in passing, though despite the froideur you must be known as a firm admirer. Your old instructor Robert Tailour—now gone to join his forefathers— had been a go-between in supplying you with some choice lessons from that quarter, but you have had none for long now. Is it already then four years since you worked through those strange violin setts, so wildly unlike Coprario's, with your brothers-in-law Robert and young George? The two boys made a stab at the violin parts, you yourself coped on bass viol, Elizabeth took the organ, on those occasions when she was spared from her household duties to receive them, as they were allowed leave from Oxford or from home in the White Horse Vale, to visit you in Twickenham. The lessons had shown a fiery talent; rough-shod in the modern way, but harshly seductive. How will he measure up to his own standard, in works for the less modish viols and organ? Of the five-part fantasy setts he has recently devised, the small band of waiting enthusiasts has heard no more than a rumour, since none has yet been divulged for love or money. Even more remarkable then for him to branch into six-part music: nothing on that scale has trickled out of the Private Music in the last twelve years, the whole period of the king's personal rule without Parliament. You had thought it unlikely to hear more, to follow pieces like those by Peerson and Coleman that your old uncle put you through. The occasional all too infrequent lesson has come by from the hand of Jenkins, though even he has not added of late to the stock. The reason for this change is hard to fathom. Royal servants certainly have risen in esteem since they founded their academy five years ago, but it has not made the music any the easier to come by. With this new confidence, will they hoard their music faster than ever?

Your mind has wandered. The entry, 'Cease, warring thoughts', has

3

drawn to a close; voices bow to the company and retreat; theorbo-players and violins alike hasten to render up their instruments to their boys, who have brought on freshly-tuned viols. It is an imposing group of skilled masters that makes obeisance to the quality, then settles on stools around the organist (you recognise Giles Tomkins of old) and his bellows-blower. The first sett of lessons to be played is in g sol re ut with a flat, consonant with the previous vocal part of the meeting. It will begin with a pavan— how long since you have heard one in six parts? There is a surprise member of the consort, since the bass violist led on to play opposite the composer himself is a senior master of music, but no member of the Private Music: it is John Jenkins, in person, who must be back in town from one of his sojourns tutoring a country family. (He dresses in a sad cloth, but wears no man's livery.) It is a mark of respect for him to be invited, and equally for him to accept the request to play, on this strange afternoon. What is now to be attempted will likely resemble nothing you have ever heard before, you are inclined to think; nor are you proved wrong.

****

A historical capriccio like the foregoing, limply as it reads, is justifiable on one ground: the ack of evidence, other than sheer intuition, to come to grips with a very perplexing body of music. It is not an elaborate tease, since the persons mentioned existed, and most other individual facts can be borne out by record (except for the spangles on the ceiling-drape in the Cockpit Theatre). Naturally, though, the details are fanciful that concern personal relations, and (more vitally) invent wholesale a type of concert-going, in order to bring William Lawes, Robert Herrick and John Jenkins together in Whitehall one fateful spring, in the company of the narrator (a minor figure, but a real amateur and collector of music whom the reader will be required to meet again in Chapter V). On that level, the era is past recall. Why it is that so little can be resurrected to inform us about the original circumstances surrounding performance of some of the great chamber music of the 17th century, in London of the 1630s, towards the

4

end of the uneasy peace that ended in open warfare between Charles I and his subjects, is a multiplex conundrum. It is especially knotty in respect of the fairly ample record for the non-musical (especially literary) arts, and of the glaring historical scrutiny that has succeeded in laying bare every motive of the actors great and small in the time's political events. It involves by extension the whole of the large chamber repertoire, performed on strings predominantly, with a variety of continuo instruments, that had previously developed under Charles and his father James I. How and where the music was performed—even if it should be performed—how commissioned, and why composed in the very singular forms it took, are questions seemingly outside the scope of a methodology that restricts itself to the measurable. To that extent the remarks in the following survey fall quite intentionally between stools: they touch variously on procedures, models, to some extent performance practice and the contemporary reception of the music, but not to the extent of pretending to exact or comprehensive scholarship. The history of the century's chamber music is yet to be written, and what follows cannot claim to be a substitute for it. To give an accurate and exhaustive account of that period would need a far less brilliant pen than mine, to adopt a remark by Max Beerbohm; equally, trying to shed light on it informally risks exasperating as much as it enlightens. There is, though, ample room for setting a ball rolling with a personal view (arising from an involvement with the music at the artisan level of establishing sound musical texts for performance) that can contribute to appreciation of the most significant part of this rewarding composer's output in its context. It is unabashedly an externalist view, since analyses of form are to many readers rarely satisfying except in carefully defined situations; and since little about the fantasy repertoire is yet clear, it would be especially unprofitable to attempt comment in those terms.

The chief recourse for following the course of the argument is to two editions by the writer: they make available the whole of William Lawes' fantasies and dances for five to six viols and organ, also the 'Royall Consort', dance-suites for performance primarily on a mixed ensemble of violins and viols, in two distinct versions. The first of these editions was published by Faber Music (London, 1979) as William Lawes, *Consort Sets in Five and Six Parts*, and the second has been published to coincide with this study by Fretwork Editions (London and Bermuda, 1995). Grateful acknowledgement is made to both publishers for permitting continual quotation from them. References to musical text and barring are from these editions: failing access to them, a generous helping may be consulted in the pioneering selection by Murray Lefkowitz in the *Musica Britannica* series (London, 1963; 2/1971), though barring in all the fantasies will be found to be at variance. As well as referring to these editions, the footnotes and bibliography try to take account of as many relevant performing editions as possible; some may well be omitted in oversight or ignorance. Eclectically, anything else with bearing on the subject is also listed, favouring the accessible. Examples of other music given involve on occasion silent emendation of questionable original readings, and adaptation from non-standard clefs. For further information on the whole period, and ample references, there is an admirably comprehensive and up-to-date bibliography in *Music in Britain: The Seventeenth Century*, ed. Ian Spink (Oxford, 1992). The pieces by Lawes all have an individual number in the Viola da Gamba Society's *Thematic Index* (Dodd 1980–92), on the system of which the editions mentioned are based, and to which this discussion makes frequent reference: nos. 1–67 for the dances of the Royall Consort, and 68–100 for the viol consorts (a more miscellaneous numbering attaches to Lawes' earlier four-part aires, which are included in the Royall Consort edition mentioned above). A roman numbering I–X for the viol-consort setts is also used, as in the published edition, to head sections; the setts of the Royal Consort bear arabic numbering 1–10. Normative spellings like 'fantasy', 'pavan', have generally been used here, though the editions referred to maintain the composer's own characterful spelling. For brevity, major keys are referred to in italic capital letters, minor keys in minuscule (so that 'key of *a*' refers to *a* minor).

Most comments are intended to be complementary to, rather than to replace, what has already been dealt with thoroughly elsewhere. The chief biographical and general study is still the monograph by Murray Lefkowitz, *William Lawes* (1960), which is updated by Professor Lefkowitz's entry on the composer in *Grove 6* (1980) and its forthcoming revision, and to which the interested reader will no

6

doubt refer. An attempt to supplement the experience of listeners without access to the main editions is a large aim of what is said below. All the viol consorts can be heard in recorded form at the time of publication, though a complete discography is not included here; the Royall Consort too is now beginning to reach a wider public through recordings. How highly to rate this music is a subjective and unrewarding question which will be side-stepped somewhat; but that it does deserve attention and respect is not simply the conviction of a small (if expanding) coterie which has participated in its rediscovery, but the experience of a growing number of performers who, with the benefits of refounded conservatoire traditions for the authentic instruments, have taken it on themselves to interpret the music afresh and bring it to greater notice. That this is written at all is largely owing to them and the help they have provided. There are also personal debts to be acknowledged, to a variety of people who have been willing to discuss ideas, which I hope are registered in adequate form beneath. In especial, many insights have been gleaned from Christine and Layton Ring, June and Francis Baines and their lifelong involvement with the music, which it would be churlish not to record. Considerable material and technical assistance in putting together drafts in book form was given by Drs Stuart Carr and Jenny Leonard, to whom I am most grateful. The principal debt owed as often is to family; to parents for support and encouragement, and especially to Emily, Tessa, Alice and Jane, for what can only be called forbearance.

I
Aire

The paths opening before a professional musician, during the short
life of William Lawes, 1602–1645, must have resembled the Choice of
Heracles, in the famous fable of Prodicus, known to every 17th-cen-
tury schoolboy. That great hero was confronted by the two imposing
female figures of Virtue and Pleasure (no prize for identifying the
frumpy one), urging the pursuit of very diverse goals in life, and
offering prospects of correspondingly dissimilar earthly rewards. The
age was one of renewal and metamorphosis in art-music, to which
Lawes contributed as fully as any other English composer; a conti-
nent-wide shift transformed a Renaissance motet-culture into one
suited to a more secular society, in which dance-idioms submerged
old categories and launched new baroque forms. It is no surprise that
Lawes prospered by his gift for the new: that he kept faithful to the
older fantasy style of chamber music for larger forces of five to six
strings and organ continuo, after most composers had turned away
from it, is the surprise. It poses a tough question since it is just as
hard to say what moved any composer of the earlier 17th century, in
the generation preceding Lawes, to devote time to complex musical
forms that enjoyed limited circulation and appeal.

There is no patronising a culture that created Tudor drama, Stuart
metaphysical verse, post-Commonwealth Miltonic epic, to name only
the chiefer indications of its literary stature. But placing great chamber music in this social setting, and crediting the possibility that this
age was just as self-aware in creating its musical canons, seems to be
more of a problem than for the explicit and verbal arts. And yet the
parochial musical traditions in England, as much as anywhere else in
Europe, had long been evolving, and included a polyphonic instrumental repertoire existing by 1530, the time that such abstract pieces
are first known in print; certainly, predating religious reformation.
By hook or crook, its forms evolved steadily, through all the times of
disruption, including civil war, until they flared out for the last time
in 1680, in the enigmatic 'fantazias' of 21-year-old Purcell. During
the period of maximum output, say 1605–1625, they equalled or

outshone vocal music as a repository for composers' most deeply felt work.

A shift from vocal to instrumental techniques, perhaps from those where rules can be formulated to others where they can best be wordlessly acquired—and then the sooner outrun by the fingers— was in evidence by the mid-16th century. Coloured by a long-standing preference for sumptuous textures, such as found in the votive antiphons of the Eton Choirbook (most written by 1502), it combined in the island's music with other traits, like toleration of dissonance and the willingness to compromise the hegemony of strict imitative counterpoint, to produce the chamber-music tradition. Given this background it is unsurprising if acceptance of new baroque continuo techniques was lukewarm at first, and tempered no doubt by suspicion of anything from the torrid south. Partly because Continental traditions of learned academies never quite caught on in England, there was something provisional or empirical in its adaptation to change. In this way, the achievements of every great composer up to the time of Purcell are rendered more distinctive by the limitations, which encouraged diversity. The process of redefining oneself, by reference to past experience, and to expectations of what is to be, applies to none of us more than musicians who (more than any other artists) inhabit that crucial gap between past and future, the fleeting moment. If music in recorded form is, even in the most peaceful of times, transience imperfectly captured, it makes especially difficult the task of defining its nature in ages of rapid transition or breakdown, and may, one hopes, excuse the roundabout path taken here.

The known biographical details of William Lawes' career are as scanty as for any player-composer of the age, and for similar reasons. Owing to the guild system, artisans were apprenticed for a long period, customarily between the ages of 17 and 24, until being admitted to mystery of their trade. Until then, rules bound them from plying their skills (and hence earning real money) separately from their masters. Any performing beforehand, and *a fortiori* composing, would have been pointless for budding performers. This seems to be the reason for the apparent latency period of great talents, like that of John Jenkins, for example, and their rise to prominence in such a traceless way. And so, from the largely anecdotal evidence that tends to emerge posthumously, are pieced together the legends.

It is hard to know what the story amounts to, that William, youngest of three musical boys in the family of a lay vicar at Salisbury Cathedral and already showing talent, was apprenticed to John Coprario at the expense of Edward Seymour, 2nd Earl of Hertford. The earl was undoubtedly a connoisseur of technique; he is reputed by John Aubrey to have said 'that if he were to earne his living, he had no way, but that of a Fidler: & thus were severall great persons bred in those daies'.[1] If he picked out William for encouragement, it suggests a date of 1619 for his induction, and so not an extended period of association with this noble family, since the aged earl died in 1621. Coprario followed in 1626, in the disease-ridden years of the mid-'20s that saw off a swathe of the older talent through one cause or another—Byrd, Dowland in the senior generation; the junior including Orlando Gibbons, Thomas Lupo (I, who is nowadays credited with most or all of the consort music under the name) and Alfonso Ferrabosco II.

By this time Lawes would have been fully-fledged as a performer, omnicompetent on all instruments, as his elder brother Henry later boasted on his behalf.[2] But composing was another matter; jam, on top of the day-to-day, bread-and-butter work of providing background music to the social events of the well-to-do. (Did they pay for the supply of fresh compositions as such, as opposed to hiring performers who extemporised? One has one's doubts.) The country gentry to some extent continued to maintain household musicians, even if patterns of expenditure were altering and reducing the size of retinues.[3] At this time, as indeed ever since the late middle ages, London was unrivalled as the only suitable arena for performers of standing. How to get there must have occupied the thoughts of many a player. Lawes was of course lucky in that he had been preceded: one elder

[1] Modern text in Aubrey (1972), 114. Lefkowitz (1960) is unsuperseded as a biographical and general study of Lawes; see also Evans (1941).
[2] 'Neither was there any Instrument then in use, but he compos'd to it so aptly, as if he had only studied that' W. and H. Law es (1648), sig. A4, epistle 'To The Reader'.
[3] Stone (1966); Woodfill (1953) is the chief study of musicians' working conditions. See also Hulse (1991).

brother, Henry, had done well with the aristocracy; the other, John, found his niche as a singing-man in Westminster Abbey. We are heavily dependent on musical sources—surviving partbooks—to give an indication of how William's training launched him into the more uncertain world of an instrumentalist player-composer; for there is no direct indication that at this early stage he was readily accepted amongst the elevated clique of royal musicians, or favoured in some way as a natural successor to Coprario.

The Shirley family of Staunton Harrold in Leicestershire is most notorious these days for the parish church that Sir Robert foolhardily took on himself to erect in 1653, during the Protectorate of Oliver Cromwell, a forlorn-hope monument to high-church Anglicanism. Less for this than for another type of masonry, the persistent dabbling in royalist plots, he quite properly ended up in the Tower of London. A glance at the church silverware, now in the Victoria and Albert Museum, gives a further cause for raised eyebrows, as does a recidivist Catholic strain in the immediate family through his mother Lady Dorothy (d. 1636), daughter of the Earl of Essex. This was by no means the most flamboyant branch of the family (others included blatant adventurers and poseurs, like the contemporary Sir Anthony, self-appointed ambassador to the Sophy of Persia), but it was colourful enough, and apparently the musical one.[4] The Ferrers Songbook, now New York Public Library, Drexel MS 4041, witnesses the liking of Sir Robert, 4th bart., and his older brother Charles for the playhouse song repertoire current in the late 1630s (the book's title comes about because the family was raised to the peerage with the earldom of Ferrers; though the story that the 18th-century black sheep, Laurence, 4th Earl, was able to claim a silken cord by noble privilege when he was hanged seems to be mythical).[5]

A slightly earlier witness to their parents' love of music comes in consort partbooks, for two to six instruments, written out largely in the youthful hand of William Lawes: the Shirley partbooks, now in the British Library, Add. 40657–61. Such novice work must at least partly predate his coming to full estate, about 1626; and fittingly, the

[4] See Shirley (1841); Davies (1967); Oman (1957), part 3 ch. 3. Porter (1994), 122 discusses Staunton church in the context of rebuilding after the war.
[5] Cutts (1964).

bulk of this copying is made up of the fantasy fodder of the Jacobean period, in five to six parts, that seems to have run to seed around the time that Charles I succeeded his father in 1625. There is no more than a middling-sized portion, in not especially authoritative form, of the works by Coprario one would expect, alongside pieces by the usual crew of Ferrabosco II, Lupo I, John Ward and lesser lights: the contents are given in tabular form at the chapter's end. Also of interest is a group of untexted Italian madrigals, all in five parts. These betray less a stylistic origin for the English type of fantasy, as it had been evolving in Coprario's time, than a cultural affinity; ascending from Vecchi's light canzonet-type to the sublime, in Marenzio's setting of Petrarch's 'Solo e pensoso', *Libro IX* a5 (1599) no. 12, and Monteverdi. It was a selection that seems to have been passed around more or less as a MS anthology, occurring with variations in other similar collections.

What else the Shirley books do is mark the first steps of Lawes, as a writer of small-scale aires, as one perhaps would expect. Quite early on in the process of copying he was encouraged to contribute 6 of his own little dances in the recently prevalent Tr–Tr–B style; 'triosonata', one might almost call it, except that like the term 'string-quartet' for the associated Tr–Tr–T–B style, it is an anachronistic way to describe an early baroque development, that possessed its own easy-going discursive and highly circumlocutory narrative. It had vocal rather than instrumental mannerisms; without recourse, that is, to repetition formulae and sequence for cumulative effects, but reliant on the inherited pathos of madrigalian contours. It followed naturally out of the late-Renaissance large-scale textures in which antiphony and dialogue flourished, encouraged by the antithetical mode of secular poetic texts. (The way had been clearly signposted by changes in purely musical textures, as found in vocal and instrumental music by Coprario and Ferrabosco; and it just needed a gentle push to turn it into a norm.)

Though far from pretentious, as seen from the alman that comes first of these dances (see Ex. 1), this début by Lawes is marked by its own character, and brings to the fore a conundrum about original scoring. These pieces are clearly signposted in the Shirley books, in the composer's hand, as three-part aires, yet some surface in later

Ex. 1: Alman (320)

copies with an idiomatic and probably authentic fourth (tenor) line. One assumes that by the second half of the 1620s budding composers were inducted routinely into Tr–Tr–B texture, since it had spread as far as quite provincial figures like Thomas Holmes of Salisbury, whose aires in this disposition Lawes copied to follow his. To some degree, then, Lawes' tenor line is a subsidiary part, even if it had been anchored in his mind's ear, in the original conception of the piece. It leads directly to an idiom where the harmonic implications of a realised continuo line can clash with abandon against the incidental detail of inner lines. Even so, the melodic language is flowing and insinuating, not far from that of (say) Jenkins in his similar four-part aires; the gestures are unradical. The real novelties are apparent in the first two bars: the uncompromising way that the trebles assert their rights against each other to the initial motif (at the key-note and at the tonal fifth reply); and the way in which the tenor underpins the tonal reply by a logical amplification which results in discord against the harmonic bass. It holds the triadic third to the end of bar 1 against a passing dominant chord in the bass, and glides up over the re-emergent third in bar 2, to produce another titillating glancing effect, of 6–4 against 5–3 on the second crotchet of the bar. Lawes was toying in minuscule with the joys of having one's cake and eating it: the creation of a simulacrum of counterpoint in a post-contrapuntal harmony. After this it hardly dares re-emerge for the rest of the piece, apart from a couple of strong chords where one treble clashes with the other in asserting a new harmonic position (bar 16, a 6–3 transformed into a dominant seventh; and the very characteristic discord in bar 22, when the alien configuration caused by line I, landing on its e" in the middle of another 6–3 chord in the G tonality, succeeds in hauling the basso line upwards to suit its purposes). This is a far cry from the functional bass of the high baroque, but has a clear taste of the Italian early baroque, Monteverdi in particular (though only if one leaves out of the equation the lucid rhythmic structures and reliance on sequential patterns that never quite caught on in England).

By the end of the first stage of copying the Shirley books, Lawes had completed an anthology of 30 three-part pieces (and comparable amounts in two and four to six parts), after which there was a lull. This will have come before February 1633, when Sir Henry Shirley, 2nd bart., died, and Lady Dorothy after a seemly interval remarried; and Lawes himself was rising to some prominence in the big world.[6] But Lawes cannot have forgotten old friends and obviously returned to the family, since at least two more separate bouts of copying can be made out, in which he concentrated on his own works: to begin with (around 1635 or so), extra three-part aires, as well as some of the four-part aires in the currently fashionable Tr–Tr–T–B scoring. At this time he also added two striking new works to the end of the five-part section, one an untitled fantasy, the other entitled 'Inñomine'; the first signs of his personal engagement with this type of repertoire, and connected possibly with his appointment to the king's Private Music.

6 See La Belle (1980) for Lady Dorothy's literary remains amongst Aston papers, now at San Marino in the Huntington Library.

14

(The later, hurried scrawl at the end of the four-part section, it has been suggested by Gordon Dodd, could be dated as late as the civil-war period when possibly Lawes was being marched through the wearisome Midland campaigns in whatever capacity he was bearing arms for the king; tramping to or from the relief of Newark, perhaps, in March 1644?) Two of the aires from the second bout, an alman and corant (nos. 103b and 339b), are variants on old war-horses that circulated as part of a sett in *g* which predates the Royall Consort proper. It appears that Lawes could write out pat the outer lines I and IV for the alman, but had to refashion from memory its less fixed subsidiary inner parts, the 2nd Treble and Tenor: hence the discrepancies in detail. With the corant a wholesale lengthening and reworking took place.

Quite apart from this prentice work for the Shirley family, it is likely that Lawes was kept busy in similar copying and of course playing for other employers. The years before he succeeded in gaining his place in 1635 in the Royal Music are tantalisingly blank; though it can be assumed that dogsbodying for other musicians already in royal service would have been a part of these untraceable activities —is it unduly cynical to see music as one of those walks of life where the bulk of the effective work is done before the security of a salaried post is gained?

In wondering how traceable the copying activities are, one turns to a very miscellaneous group of MSS. One of the two subsidiary hands that contributed to the Shirley books has been noticed in another fairly similar if earlier anthology of fantasies, together with vocal music (some by Coprario) that lies on the instrumental divide: the Ellesmere Partbooks from the collection of the Bridgewater family, well known for its patronage of Henry Lawes and John Milton.[7] Could an early calligraphic hand of William Lawes, like that which copied Coprario's six-part madrigal-fantasy 'Che mi consigli, amore?', lie here unsuspected? The likenesses are too tenuous to be sure; but one is surely on a warmer scent by looking at a copyist of the 1620s who crops up in all the places where Lawes would be expected. A keyboard (organ) part to his master Coprario's violin 'setts', which William was later to emulate and surpass, yet survives in the Royal Music (now

[7] Hamessley (1992).

15

housed in the British Library, as MS RM 24.k.3), bearing a contemporary stamp of the royal arms. It can be hard at times to be sure with an immature roundish Italianate hand where one copyist leaves off and another begins, but the likelihood that Lawes was throughout at work seems strong, to one peruser. The hand contributed to a very scrappy set of string parts now found in Oxford, Christ Church MSS Mus. 732–5, though to complicate matters the music hand (as often, elsewhere) is not always the same as the 'script' hand that provides the titling.[8] Interestingly, the spelling of the organbook for the composer's name, of 'Cooperario', which as well as an indication of contemporary pronunciation may allude to his original name (apparently 'plain John Cooper'), is repeated in another important MS where a similar, perhaps identical, hand was at work, and where some clues to Lawes' activities lie buried: the scorebook, Tenbury MS 302.

Consort Sett I: Fantazy, Playnsong (68–9)

Tenbury 302, from the collection of one of the last great 19th-century stalwarts, Sir Frederick Ouseley, by chance or no covers much of the same ground as the Shirley books for the repertoire in three to five parts. Coprario, Lupo and Marenzio are common denominators, as well as a scatter of similar pieces that could have occurred in either set. The date of its compilation seems to be by 1635: a group of four four-part fantasies by Michael East, not published till 1638, was given by the third of the copyists the date 1630.[9] The important

---

[8] These partbooks came to the hands of a contemporary collector, Sir Christopher Hatton III, probably towards the end of the 1630s when they may have been replaced by freshly copied replacements for court use; see Pinto (1990); *MB* LX, p. xvi; Charteris (1975) for contents and hands of the set.

[9] Willetts (1991) identifies the work of the various hands in Tenbury 302, and gives a table of the contents. Identity of the copyists is, though, still a matter for debate. Lawes was a good friend of John Tomkins (a member of the Chapel Royal, but also organist of Paul's), to judge by the extraordinary lament he wrote for him on his death on 27 Sept. 1638: 'Musique, the Master of thy Art is dead', found in W. and H. Lawes (1648) and GB-Ob, MS Mus. Sch. B.2, p. 101; and there is every reason to suppose that it was work that brought them together, and that Lawes was well known to musicians of Paul's amongst whom the Barnard MSS were compiled.

16

contents here are not so much the three-part aires by Lawes but the later 'ffantasie' and 'Iñomine' at the end of the five-part section, also found in the Shirley books.[10] Tantalisingly these pieces carry a 19th-century pencil annotation referring to the 'original single parts', which Ouseley may also have acquired, but now are unknown. The musical text is very similar to that in the Shirley books, as opposed to later revisions.

One does wonder why Lawes wrote these two pieces at all. He set hardly a foot in the four-part fantasy genre, which is distinct to a large extent from the repertoire in five to six parts. Between Alfonso Ferrabosco II and Henry Purcell there is a lineage that passes through Jenkins and Locke, thin-blooded enough at other times, of writers who kept alive four-part writing and the corresponding special affinity for strict counterpoint, even if its ancestry in Continental ricercar is unlikely to have been at the forefront of their minds. Here if anywhere was the *musica reservata* for the chamber musicians, if any of them desired to play absolute music: Lawes as a child of his times, the late '20s on, never supplicated as an initiate to this fraternity. It is only with hindsight that one could have known that the day of the four-part ricercar style was not over; but no-one could have foreseen the effects of war (by forcing music back to the parlour) on the shape of the repertoire. And so by the early '30s the fantasy in five to six parts too must have seemed unprofitable, to any budding composer.

All of the 'breakaway' genres pioneered in the household of Charles I while he had been Prince of Wales, it is true, had paid lip-service to fantasy form, if one can call a 'form' something of no pre-scribed shape. Works by Orlando Gibbons, involving violins no less than the seemingly more progressive experimental violin 'setts' of Coprario, qualify here.[11] All the same, a gap emerged in the later '20s which no-one was bold enough to fill, either with more music in the established vein, or in novel forms to substitute. One reason may lie in the economic disarray of the times, the disruption of trade

---

[10] Text of all the works in 5–6 parts to the organ in Lawes *Consort Sets* ed. Pinto; a previous selection in Lawes ed. Lefkowitz (1963) = *MB* XXI.
[11] See Coprario ed. Charteris (1980) = *MB* XLVI; Gibbons ed. Harper (1982) = *MB* XLVIII, for the violin setts by Coprario and the fantasies to the 'great Dooble Basse' by Gibbons, which seem apt for violin too in the treble part.

Europe-wide and retrenchment by patrons.[12] The older contemporaries of Lawes whom he must have known and learned from, like Coleman, Peerson, Ives, all London-based and outside court circles to a man (apart from Coleman), wrote little or nothing new in the '30s for the larger ensemble. Contrariwise, while court musicians in the employ of Charles as Prince of Wales had freely tinkered with textures or scorings, the leap to new forms to suit the new instrumentations had eluded them. It is doubly strange in the climate of the times, when one compares the inventiveness of the Italian baroque, working on continuo repetition-forms like chaconne and passacaglia. To some extent this explains the success of the dance-suite in the reign of Charles, which partly through the influence of his wife Henrietta Maria, sister to Louis XIII, witnessed a rage for all things Gallic including clothing. (It took the mid-century upheavals, and the return of Charles I's wandering son after the Restoration, to give a jolt to ingrained musical thought-habits.) Do Lawes' pieces succeed, in this context, in doing anything radical?

To begin with, the title of 'In Nomine' applied to the second of the pieces is grossly misleading. Lawes later, when adding the piece in his scorebook, entitled the revised version 'On the Playnsong'; so someone may have placed a word in his ear. The plainsong had been entirely confected, probably by the composer himself, and bears no resemblance to the In Nomine *cantus firmus*. Had there been no-one around earlier to show him the ropes? The idea is hard to credit, but then one wonders what sort of continuity existed by the early '30s, after the passing of the older generation (if you except the provincial and aged Elway Bevin, who as a suspected recusant may be expected to have had some idea of the liturgical function behind his own youthful plainsong exercises). Still, there were city musicians, and those connected with St Paul's like William Cranford and Simon Ives, whom Lawes knew personally or else through their music; they wrote examples. Jenkins was, apparently sometime later, to turn his hand to a couple in six parts; and a series of inventive (if incompletely successful) fantasies by John Ward, which must belong to the period but had

---

[12] A large (and controversial) literature amongst modern historians exists on the topic; Parker and Smith (1978) gives a taste. See also Bianconi (1987) for music.

little circulation, begins with a respectable five In Nomines.[13] Perhaps, then, Lawes' frolic can be put down to an irrepressibly buoyant nature.

It must also be confessed that the whole In Nomine tradition is still shrouded in considerable mystery. One may no longer need to enquire into the first step, the taking of an excerpt from the Benedictus of John Taverner's Missa 'Gloria Tibi Trinitas', composed around 1528 during his time at Archbishop Wolsey's Cardinal College, Oxford (which was dedicated to the Trinity, and very fittingly was later incorporated into the present foundation of Christ Church), since the process of adapting vocal music for instrumental use is age-old—but why this particular episode, in a mere four parts, at the words 'In nomine domini'? And why did it become such a compositional resource? The shrewd lawyer and musical antiquarian Roger North, a pupil of Jenkins' old age, was too far removed from this tradition to claim first-hand knowledge, but he made an inspired guess that an In Nomine was demanded of apprentices as a test-piece or masterpiece before admittance to their mystery. Though not an explanation of why some composers could hardly keep their hands off the form—one thinks of the prolific Tye, or especially of the 'virtuous contention' between the émigré Alfonso Ferrabosco I, the only real foreigner to tangle with it, and his friend William Byrd (a very influential *débat* for future writers)—it may go some way to explaining the odd survival of single compositions by the otherwise negligible figures of the age (and of course the present absence of 'master-pieces' by many fine composers is no counter-argument, since one would expect considerable wastage in this area). There was a Jacobean revival of the form by Ferrabosco II and his school, including Gibbons; these were indebted thematically to the elder Ferrabosco and of course Byrd, their fresh insight being the figurate counterpoint more typical of the new fantasy. By the mid-'20s this too had, like the fantasy, run out of steam, and so an attempt by Lawes to write a *cantus firmus* piece of any sort was more isolated than at first may appear.

---

[13] The so-called 'Paris' fantasies, from their occurrence uniquely in F-Pc, MS Rés.F.770; see Lawes ed. Pinto (1991) = *MB* LX, 116, and the musical text in J. Ward ed. Brookes (1993).

The piece is comparable in length to a genuine In Nomine, the fire and dash resembling (say) the zany energy in William Cranford's sole five-part example in the genre; though there similarities end. It is one of the more extreme examples of bravura in Lawes, with little thematic cohesion except the onward flow of its own argument within itself; it takes the bass part as high as ever it goes, to b' in bar 35 (tenors too reach their height for the five-part setts). There is an odd octave drop in pitch in the *cantus firmus* at mid-point, bars 29–30, for no apparent reason, and unparalleled except, oddly enough, in a four-part In Nomine by Christopher Tye written nearly a century earlier. Lawes could conceivably have known the very musical source which we rely on for acquaintance with the best part of Tye's pieces, now GB-Lbl Add. MS 31390—it was seemingly kept in Chapel Royal circles, and was known to Purcell, and after all must have been available from time to time in its long history for consultation; but that in itself is no real clue to the purpose and structure of Lawes' piece.[14]

That at any rate prepares ground for considering his first attempt at a fantasy, since the two pieces are paired. Scoring is the typical five-part Jacobean arrangement derived from madrigal, that had become normative for as long as five-part fantasies continued to be written: Tr–Tr–T–T–B (superseding Tr–A–T–Bar–B, more typical of the Elizabethan era, which survived in the earlier Jacobean chamber dance and In Nomine). The most striking thing, intentionally so, are its opening and closing passages: anvil blows of a smith determined to forge decisively. Lawes makes a habit of themes that exceed the vocalic curve of the usual fantasy 'point', which is cautious in outstretching a sixth. His thematic material is typically struck (or incised) on the fifth and octave degrees of the scale, with a glancing blow on the sixth or seventh degree before reposing on the fifth. Such themes contain within them large promises. In this case, deliberately, the 'tonal' answer in the treble actually precedes the bass statement in key. By pushing up to the seventh degree, so plaintively, it sets in motion a circular and irresoluble argument between the voices. (Ex. 2a).

---

[14] Study of Purcell's acquaintance with Add. 31390 in preparation by the writer.

Ex. 2a: Fantasy (68)

Ex. 2b: Fantasy in *g*; Sett no. 2   John Jenkins

This type of fragmented theme with a *suspirium* (crotchet rest) internally was not new; it is reminiscent of Coprario, as in his four-part fantasy, no. 6, incipit, and later in the same piece; also elsewhere in these innovative four-part pieces, such as no. 2, breves 31–5. (His six-part 'Sospirando' begins, fittingly enough, with another example.) Lawes develops its power, however, by using the silences to underline the strength of the leaps and fuel the insistence of his never-answered question, in a way foreign to Jenkins, who glides round his rests as a pivot that delivers him into a natural answer. This particular phrase, however, was striking and innovative enough to give Jenkins an idea, perhaps, in a violin work: the opening of a fantasy in *g* for treble, bass and organ (example 2b), to which there is an

21

Ex. 3: Fantasy (68)

early version

revised version

accompanying alman showing a superficial likeness to the alman grouped with Lawes' fantasy.[15]

Like the plainsong, the fantasy reveals Lawes tinkering with the basics of his counterpoint. The tenor parts in especial developed after the piece was circulated; they were freely interchanged in the later score, or their texture supplemented, and some rhythmic counterpoint strengthened as at the fantasy, bar 30 (Ex. 3). It reads like a token attempt to make these pieces more 'fantasy'-like; more close-textured after the pattern of Ferrabosco and Jenkins. If so, it was a passing mood before Lawes struck out more independently. The points used in the middle episodes are not so highly characterised, and the development of ideas in distinct sections is almost desultory; but the feeling of agitation and indecision is perhaps intentional, owing to the key feeling of g, which implied anguish for Lawes (whose response to key was as strong as for any composer in the later part of the century). In fact the force and ease of the development must have augured well for the future to any listener, and laid the seeds in Lawes' mind for what was to follow after an interval. A radical reshaping of fantasy texture, if not form, was not at this point in his mind.

The 'missing years' may (or may not) have involved foreign travel; the more distinguished class of musician like Coprario did go beyond the seas, as travelling companions or in personal retinues of

[15] Jenkins ed. Ashbee (1991).

the moderately well-to-do.There is extant a letter from William, 3rd Earl of Pembroke to his cousin Lord Herbert of Cherbury requesting him to accommodate the bearer, a lutenist previously 'entertain'd' by Prince Charles for his 'rare playing on the Lute', who was 'desirous to spend some time in france, for the bettring of his play, & making him fitter for the Prince's service' (dated 10 November, no year; but at some time 1619–24, the period of Cherbury's embassage).[16] There is of course no reason to assume this protégé was the young William; but if not, then all the more reason to ponder on how he will not have been the only fish in the sea, scouring for the opportunities to better himself that depended on this type of personal noble patronage. Experience of Paris would explain the speed with which Lawes took up the innovation of Parisian lutenists just before 1630, which more than anyone else he was responsible for domiciling in England: nascent suite-form, in the baroque string of alman–corant–saraband (to employ his own usual spellings).

Undoubtedly he is to be associated most with the lute in these earlier years, for as a singer to the lute as much as a bowed-string player he apparently was remembered. Mildmay Fane, Earl of Westmorland, ranked him with Nicholas Lanier, Master of the Music, and Jacques ('English') Gaultier, Queen Henrietta Maria's servant and premier lutenist of the age, when in his valediction, 'My Farewell to Court', he listed the pleasures he was resigning himself to foregoing:

> Gotyer [may] sail from the Clouds to catch our ears,
> And represent the harmony o' th' Spheres;
> Will. Lause excell the dying swan: Laneer
> Nick it with Ravishments from touch of Lyre,[17]

Robert Herrick's epicedium for Lawes as published in Hesperides associated him equally with lute, viol and voice (in that order), when naming the objects struck dumb by his death; which suggests that as a self-accompanied singer and lyra-violist he was most remembered.

[16] Burwell Tutor (1974) intr. by Robert Spencer, citing Shakespeare Birthplace Trust Records Office no. 78/1.
[17] Fane (1648) ii. 160–1.

Other laments too focus on the voice—Robert Heath made the association with Orpheus and his lyre, and made comparison with the ability of Pythagoras to appease 'a mad-brain'd multitude' with his 'soft accents, and sweet strains'. Stock classical comparisons, perhaps; although Herrick, a careful user of tropes, also thought of Orpheus alongside of Amphion and Terpander. Of these lyre-players, only Terpander was attestably historical, and interestingly is said to have increased the strings of the lyre from four to seven—shades of the new French *accords*, and the extra diapason strings of the eleven- and twelve-course lute that were employed during Lawes' time in the Private Music of the king. John Tatham began his little tribute with the words

> Who says *Will Lawes* is dead? had not his *breath*
> *Virtue* enough to *charm* the *Spleen* of *Death?*

which again seems to refer to the vocal gifts.[18] John Jenkins—and who a better judge?—gave first place to these same aspects of his performing abilities, the lute and possibly voice, in quite excessive tropes:

> he/ who with harmonious numbers tame could keep
> the Nemean Lion, force the Panther weep,
> melt the hard marble; he who nimbly hurl'd
> Seraphick raptures, and so charm'd the world,
> as if th'incircled aire grew proud t'aspire,
> and court the Spheres with musique of his Lyre.

John Cobb, domestic musician to the executed Archbishop William Laud, and a Chapel Royal member, thought of William for his vocal music:

> In his just proportioned songs there might you find
> his soule convers'd with heav'n, heaven with his mind.[19]

---

[18] Heath (1650), 9–10; T[atham] (1650), 111–12.
[19] Cobb and Jenkins both in W. and H. Lawes (1648): 'Deare *Will* is dead, *Will Lawes*, whose active braine' and 'Why in this shade of night? *Amice*, say'.

24

Aurelian Townshend, as cited by Lefkowitz, was seemingly the only elegist to make a distinction between the gifts of the two brothers Henry and William, by assigning them different (if unspecified) spheres; one sounded the 'depth of music', the other the 'height' (which is far from establishing a distinct vocal–instrumental divide between their roles, though it suggests it).[20] It may, though, be significant that when Sir John Berkenhead, a veteran of the propaganda machine in the civil-war Oxford court, prefaced some encomiastic verse to Henry Lawes' *Second Book of Ayres* (1655), he paid tribute in passing to the dead 'glorious *Brother* ... Whose *Coffin* is each *Chest of Viols* now'.

In whatever manner William first made his name, his facility for dance was not to be overborne. There is a special drive to the aires by him that began now to accumulate. Though Playford's printed dance collections for Tr–B are mid-century, they rescue (sometimes uniquely) music of the preceding 30 years, just as much as do MS collections like that of Edward Lowe, a native of Salisbury (like the Lawes brothers), who rose to the position of Professor of Music at Oxford in 1661, succeeding John Wilson, the virtuoso lutenist and another colleague of the Lawes brothers before the wars. A taste or two of their freakish, disjointed unpredictability will have to suffice, though the energy and casual assurance of even these light pieces deserves to be encountered whole (Ex. 4a: Alman 256, 2nd strain, from Lowe's MSS; 4b: Saraband 268 from Playford, 1662).

The other dimension to Lawes' most public face, the performing, was the lyra-viol. By a quirk of survival, the lute-music of generations of native performers, from Ferrabosco II and Jenkins to players of the Commonwealth period like John Rogers, apparently composed in profusion, has totally or almost totally vanished, when the often slighter lyra repertoire has fared decidedly better because copied for amateur recreation. Though outside the present scope, it is obvious that the constantly shifting registers of the solo lyra spurred on Lawes in developing his melodic language; and that he was not the only composer whose harmonic thinking was freed by tablature from the fetters of a conventional stave-based mentality (one thinks

---

[20] Townshend, ibid., quoted by Lefkowitz (1960), 22.

Ex. 4a: Alman (256)

Ex. 4b: Saraband (268)

of lute-works, by Cuthbert Hely and Wilson, that do survive, for extended examples of dissonance technique). Many of the pieces are trifles, jottable down anywhere: the flyleaf of his autograph songbook, for example, bears a corant and two sarabands in the harpway sharp tuning, the first of them with a very similar opening to aire no. 48 from the Royall Consort.[21] Elsewhere more impressive collections of lyra consorts by Lawes survive, though only complete in one source: GB-Och 725–7 contains, alongside works by colleagues like Simon Ives and Robert Tailour, six pieces by Lawes for three viols: two fantasies and a pavan, each grouped loosely with a lighter dance. This is

[21] No listing to date for these three small pieces in Dodd (1980–92).

a fraction only, about a fifth, of what exists elsewhere by him for three lyras, now incomplete. This MS set appears to be in the composer's own hand, comparable with the early work in the Shirley books (and in other possible occurrences); one can safely date them before 1635.

Lawes' major activity in the ensemble repertoire up to the 'old version' of the Royall Consort was also close to the bread-and-butter dance category, but one where he was heading towards a very personal idiom. The main MSS for the old version offer as a sort of antechamber two chains of dances in the 'string-quartet' scoring (Tr–Tr–T–B–bc), in keys g–G, which have a central place in Lawes' output. Concordances in other anthologies where Lawes' dances have a limited appearance show that they are relatively early, in the period 1626–30, say; overlapping with the Shirley versions, but without the regular suite-form displayed in the Royall Consort. Lawes kept a place close to his heart for them, since he returned to rescore them from time to time.

The first of the sett is a pavan in g, aire 101. The numbering in the standard catalogue is unfortunately non-consecutive for these setts; but the pieces seem to have been carefully arranged as a sequence, and some of the pairings given in it are attested by the composer's rescored versions.[22] Typical of Lawes' key-usage is its prodigal scatter of diminished fourths set within the grinding casual dissonance. There is in the three strains a sequence of distress, spasms of wayward treble runs and final resolve expressed through ascending chromatics, that in total Robert Donington with habitual precision called 'grim and magnificent'. Lawes used a reduction of the piece as organ backcloth to divisions for two basses, devised some time after his court appointment, along with the alman that follows in this proto-sett (Aire 103). The other g alman of the sequence resurfaced in the five-part viol setts, almost unchanged but with a second tenor part added. The G sett was similarly quarried. The pavan–alman pair, 79–80, was reset for five viols in the key (more idiomatic for viols) of F. In these last two dances in especial there is much in the

---

[22] Dodd (1980–92) contains listings for Lawes and for the rest of the period's chamber music. Lawes ed. Pinto (1995) contains the miscellaneous aires in g–G–d as well, and further listings of sources.

Ex. 5: Pavan (79) 4-part version in G

Ex. 6: *Ibid*

long elegant treble melodies that one would term more typical of chamber music than dance proper; Lawes was refining his notions of treble duet to include more canon and antiphony, spacing the entries to reap maximum clarity but without overlightening the texture (Exx. 5–6).

Pavans in particular had almost completely ceded to the alman as chief 'social' dance, and one must assume that at least part of this repertoire was already employed for, if not a purely concert function, then some type of 'regressive listening' to grace social occasions like gaming, or of course as *Tafelmusik*. Accounts of the use of music in

the salon society of the time are regrettably few, but one of significance does survive in the memoir of her husband by the formidably
intelligent Lucy Hutchinson.[23] A daughter of Sir Allen Apsley, Lieutenant of the Tower, who had died in May 1630 after a 3-year illness,
when she was only 10, she encountered her husband-to-be about 1636
in Richmond, where she boarded for lute-lessons. He likewise was
lodging nearby for the summer, at the house of his music-master
Charles Coleman; not only for the music but for the hawking and
other gentle pastimes that flourished there, around the court of the
Prince of Wales. It was a polite finishing school; Coleman ranked almost as a gentleman in such circles.

The man being a skilled composer in music, the rest of the king's musicians
often met at his house to practise new airs and prepare them for the king;
and divers of the gentlemen and ladies that were affected with music, came
thither to hear; others that were not, took that pretence to entertain themselves with the company.

Possibly the Entertainment at Richmond for king and queen, mounted
in September 1636 on behalf of their 6-year old son Prince Charles
and composed by Coleman in association with the violinist Simon
Hopper, was at the time under rehearsal.[24] In such a setting, music-
meetings combined instrumental and vocal items with *vers de société*.
John Hutchinson's first direct experience of his future wife's qualities came from hearing a verse riposte she had made to a song previously performed; and acquaintance blossomed during this stay of
six weeks or more, during a party in Sion Gardens, for instance, where
they were chaperoned by Coleman's daughter. Any record of
Coleman's activities is welcome, since he was a prolific composer of
aires, and this has a bearing on activities by Lawes at a time when the
dance-suites that evolved into the Royall Consort must have been
taking shape over the preceding half-decade or so.

---

[23] Hutchinson (1908), 44–8.
[24] Holman (1993)

The Shirley Partbooks: GB-Lbl, Additional MSS 40657–40661

Source No.	Composer	Works	Foliation					Numeration/ comment all contents fantasies unless noted[a]
			40657	40658	40659	40660	40661	
Two-part:								
1–3 [5–8]	Jo Coperario	'Duo'	—	—	—	—	35v–32rev	1–8 (7–8 *unica*)
Three-part:								
1–4	Tho: Lupo		2–3v	2–3v	—	2–3v	—	2–3, 10, 13
5–8	Chetwoode		4–5	4–5	—	4–5	—	1–4 (*unica*)
9	William Lawes	'Ayres'	5v	5v	—	5v	—	320*
10	William Lawes		5v	5v	—	5v	—	321*
11	William Lawes		6	6	—	6	—	75
12	William Lawes		6	6	—	6	—	226
13	William Lawes		6v	6v	—	6v	—	83*
14	William Lawes		7	7	—	7	—	206*
15–17	Tho: Holmes	'Ayres'	7v–8	7v–8	—	7v–8	—	1–3 (*unica*)
18–27	Jo: Coprario		8v–13	8v–13	—	8v–13	—	1–6*, 7–8, 9–10*
28–9	Tho: Holmes	Pavan (*F*)	13v	13v	—	13v	—	
	Tho: Holmes	Almaine (*d*)	13v	13v	—	13v	—	
30	Nich:[olas] Guy		14	14	—	14	—	(*unicum*)
[31]	[William Lawes]	[Aires]	14v	14v	—	14v	—	227(*unicum*)[b]
[32]	[William Lawes]		14v	14v	—	14v	—	207(*unicum*)

Source No.	Composer	Works	Foliation					Numeration/comment
			40657	40658	40659	40660	40661	
[33]	[William Lawes]		15	15	—	15	—	342c
[34]	[William Lawes]		15	15	—	15	—	208(*unicum*)
	[*unfilled*]		15v	15v	—	15v	—	
	[*unnumbered ruled folia: quantity*]		[2]	[1]		[2]		

Four-part:

Source No.	Composer	Works	40657	40658	40659	40660	40661	Numeration/comment
1–6	'Jo: Ward'		16v–18	16v–18	2–4v	16v–18	—	1–2, 4–5, 3, 6
7	'Tho: Lupo'		19	19	5	19	—	8*
8	'Tho: Foord'	[Aire]	19v	19v	5v	19v	—	
9	[Sandrin^d]	'Dulcis Memoriae'	20	20	6	20	—	3
10	Simon Ives		20v–21	20v–21	6v–7	20v–21	—	3
11	Simon Ives		21v–22	21v–22	7v–8	21v–22	—	4
12–17	Coprario		22v–25	22v–25	8v–11	22v–25	—	1–6*
18–19	'Alfonso' [Ferrabosco II]		25v–26	25v–26	**11v–12**	25v–26	—	13, 15
20	'Doc:Bull'	'Aires'	26v	26v	12v	26v	—	'Dorick' fantasy
21	'W.J:Lawes'		27	27	13	27	—	110e
22	'W.J:Lawes'		27v	27v	13v	27v	—	306
25 [*sic*]	'W.J:Lawes'		28	28	14	28	—	336(*unicum*)
26	'W.J:Lawes'		28v	28v	14v	28v	—	109f
27	'W.J:Lawes'		29	29	15	29	—	318(*unicum*)
	[*unfilled*]		29v	—	—	—	—	
[28]	William Lawes	Aire	—	29v	15v	29v	—	319(*unicum*)
[29–30]	William Lawes	[Aires]	30	30	16	30	—	337(*unicum*)103bg
[31]	William Lawes	[Aire]	30v	30v	16v	30v	—	339b
	[*unnumbered ruled folia: quantity*]		[10]	[11]	[10]	[8]	—	

Source No.	Composer	Works	Foliation					Numeration/comment
			40657	40658	40659	40660	40661	

Five-part:

Source No.	Composer	Works	40657	40658	40659	40660	40661	Numeration/comment
1–6	Tho:Lupo		*31–33v*	*31–33v*	*17–19v*	*31–33v*	*2–4v*	11, 5, 12–13, 1–2
7	'Cla:Mounteverdie'	[O come e gran]	34	34	20	34	5	*Libro III* (1595) no.2
8	'Cla:Mounteverdie'	[Là tra'l sangue]	34	34	20	34	5	*II* (1595) no.9
9–14	Coprario		34v–37	34v–37	20v–23	34v–37	5v–8	45–6, 5, 35, 49, 48
15–16	Ward		37v–38	37v–38	23v–24	37v–38	8v–9	2, 4
17	[Ward]	[Cor mio]	*38v*	*38v*	*24v*	*38v*	*9v*	Meyer no.12h
18	William White	[Diapente]	39	39i	25	39	10	
19	'Luca Maurenzio'	'Arda pur'	39v	39v	25v	39v	10v	*VII* (1595) no.11
20	[Marenzio]	'Rimanti in pace'	39v	39v	25v	39v	10v	*VI* (1594) no.17
21	[Marenzio]	'Ond'ei di mortie'	40	40	26	40	11	*VI* no.18
22	[Marenzio]	'Caro dolce'	40	40	26	40	11	*III* (1582) no.2
23	[Marenzio]	'Che se tu'	40v	40v	26v	40v	11v	*VI* i
24	'Horatio Vocchi'	'Clorind'hai vinto'	40v	40v	26v	40v	11v	*I* (1589)
25	'Monteuerdio'	'Saura tenere herbette'	41	41	27	41	12	*III* (1592) no.3
26	[Marenzio]	'Deh poi ch'era'	41v	41v	27v	41v	12v	*VII* (1595) no.1
27	'Be:Pallauicino'	'Com vivrò'	41v	41v	27v	41v	12v	*VI* (1600) no.1
28	'Luca Maurenzio'	'Quell' augellin'	42	42	28	42	13	*VII* (1595) no.2
29	[Lupo]	[Miserere]	42	—	—	—	—	Psalm 85, 2nd setting
30	'Alfonso Ferrabosco' [II]	'Pauen'	42v	42v	28v	42v	13v	no.1 (Dovehouse)
31	'Luca Maurenzio'	[Solo e pensoso]	43	43	29	43	14	*X* (1599) no.12*
32	William Lawes	[Fantasy]	43v	43v	29v	43v	14v	68*
33	William Lawes	'Innomine'	44	44	30	44	15	69*
—	[Lupo]	(all books) *[unfilled verso]*						
—		*[unnumbered ruled folia: quantity]*	[23]	[22]	[24]	[21]	[17]k	

Source No.	Composer	Works	Foliation					Numeration/comment
			40657	40658	40659	40660	40661	

Six-part:

Source No.	Composer	Works	40657	40658	40659	40660	40661	Numeration/comment
1	Tho:Lupo		45	45	31	45	25	1
2	'Alfonso' [Ferrabosco II]		45v	45v	31v	45v	25v	2
3–4	'Will:White'		46r–v	46r–v	32r–v	46r–v	26r–v	3–4
5	'Jo:Warde'	In Nomine	47	47	33	47	27	2
6	'Alfonso' [Ferrabosco II]		47v	47v	33v	47v	27v	3
7	[Ferrabosco II]	In Nomine	48	48	34	48	28	1
8–9	Will:White		**48v–9**	48v–9	34v–5	48v–9	28v–9	1–2
10–11	[William White]		49v–50	49v–50	35v	49v–50	29v–30	6,5^l
12	Coprario		50v	50v	—	50v	30v	2
	[unnumbered ruled folia: quantity]		[25]	[17]	[0]	[23]	[23]^m	

a Contents all copied by William Lawes, except for folio numbers in *italic* (Hand B) or **bold** (Hand C). Hand B here is the Hand D of the Ellesmere Partbooks, now San Marino, Huntington Library, EL 25A 46–51: see Hamessley (1992). All asterisked items concord with Tenbury MS 302. All 5-part untexted madrigals concord with GB-Och, MSS Mus. 2/403–8/436 except for Marenzio, 'Solo e pensoso'.

b Nos. [31–4] in a later style of hand, perhaps c.1635 and the time of Tenbury MS 302.

c See Charles Coleman, aire no. 314 for an adaptation, Tr–A–B instead of 2Tr–B as in Lawes' original.

d *Alias* Pierre Regnault: see Dobbins (1969–70).

e Also in 40659, f. 7, crossed out; minor variants. This section c.1635 or later. See Ch. V for discussion of a version of this piece (in *c* instead of *d*) and of source no. 26 (aire no. 109) in the autograph scorebook, Mus. Sch. B.2.

f See preceding note *e* for a version of this piece in the autograph score.

g Very late hand: 1640s?   h Excluded from Dodd (1980–92).   i Hand B, apart from first 7 semibreves in hand C.

j 2a parte of 'Deh Tirsi'.   k Later (19th-cent.) additions, ff. [16v] *et seq.* (psalm-tunes, *etc.*).

l F. 36r–v missing in Add. 40659 (Tenor).   m Later additions on f. 31 inv. For ff. 32–35v see 2-part works, *supra*.

II
Royall Consort

For a work that was the prototype of the dance-suite in England, and must have enjoyed enormous prestige in its own day, the Royall Consort has proved elusive. A fair number of contemporary sources (ten chief ones) survive, in varying states of dilapidation; comparison of them shows that even where they can be grouped together textually they diverge enough to give cause for assuming a very varied larger background of antecedent copies, that have now disappeared (like Sir Peter Leycester's for example).[1] The work stayed in the repertoire from the 1630s until the 1680s at least; though for all that, there is little mention of it surviving from its own time. As suites composed largely in alman–corant–saraband sequences, which stand at the head of what became the classic form for the baroque period as a whole, it is the Royall Consort, rather than the more esoteric consort setts, that will have caught the public ear. It could for example be these setts of dances that Anthony Wood had in mind, when he included in his MS jottings on composers, about half a century on, an opinion of Lawes. Probably derived from an informant, since little native judgement of his own existed, it was favourable in the main apart from a proviso to the effect that 'to indulge the ear—he broke sometimes ye rules of mathematicall composition'.[2]

Some of the blame for later neglect of this particular music, and failure to appreciate its importance, can be imputed to Charles Burney's influential *General History of Music*, where the animadversions on William Lawes, his brother Henry, and the whole Caroline crew, may be too well known to need repeating in full. To an extent Burney had done his homework that resulted in this hatchet-job, when summing up the Royall Consort as 'one of the most dry, aukward, and unmeaning compositions I ever remember to have had the trouble of scoring'.[3] A scrupulous investigator, he had tried to be

[1] See Leicester (1953) for a library catalogue of now dispersed and lost items.
[2] GB-Ob Wood MS D.19.(4) f. 83.
[3] Burney (1776–89), ii. 309.

fair and examine the work before proceeding to judgement. The study-extracts for instrumental works mentioned by him, which might have shown what he scored, do not survive; but the 17th-century source for the Royall Consort that he possessed does, as GB-Lbl, Add. 10445. This incomplete set of three partbooks offered an inadequate Tr–Tr–B shard of the five to six parts needed for a just view. Duty once satisfied, Burney was not predisposed to tolerance, in the hanging-judge critical manner that is most familiar from his equally robust-minded friend Samuel Johnson. He had around the same time made a perusal of Playford's very comprehensive song anthology, *Select Musicall Ayres and Dialogues* (1653), to the detriment of his blood pressure; the resulting near-apoplexy gave rise to a long doggerel verse in a letter of 10–12 November 1783 to his correspondent, the Rev. Thomas Twining, showing how his patience had been exhausted (a relevant excerpt only, from a much longer tirade):

> The renown'd Harry <u>Lawes</u>
> You will find has his flaws,
> For his Treble's Psalmodic
> & Base immethodic.
> While <u>William</u>'s too rude
> To be patiently chew'd;
> But since knock'd on the head
> There's no more to be said.[4]

There is of course more to be added; but any inkling of what it was had to wait for the flair of Arnold Dolmetsch in picking out music of consequence. Rediscovery in any form of the Royall Consort in performance is barely a century old, and owes an unquantifiable amount to Dolmetsch's courage in conducting researches against the tug of received opinion, as he branched out from transcriptions made from Royal College and British Museum sources in London.[5] Apart

---

[4] Burney ed. Ribeiro (1991); see also transcript in Grant (1983).
[5] Campbell (1975), 68, 79, records a Tuesday evening concert at AD's Dulwich home, 'Dowlands', reviewed in *The Times*, 18 Feb. 1894, where a suite from the Royall Consort was played: 'beautiful ... the treatment of parts is always interesting and not seldom effective'.

from disciples of 'AD' like Gerald Hayes, few others before the pioneering work of Murray Lefkowitz (at the mid-point of the 20th century) found a positive word for the music.[6] What Burney cannot have known from his own fragmentary copies (which furthermore were partial, containing under half the 67 pieces) is the crowning glory of the setts, never hitherto available in print: the late-added fantasies and pavans, written in six real parts for the unusually specific combination of two violins, two bass viols and two theorbos. Before Lefkowitz, the complex process of rescoring through which Lawes put the entire collection was little understood, and even now leaves something to be desired.

Lawes began with 'orders' (possibly extended ones in d–D, as will emerge) in the same 'string-quartet' scoring as his shorter g–G setts. At this stage there is no proof that a differentiation into setts as such had occurred; smaller groups containing a viable minimum of each dance-form, such as alman–alman–corant–corant–saraband, could have been the nuclei. At some point he decided, or else was commanded, to reshape the lot for the more adventurous Tr–Tr–B–B–bc. There evolved a sequence of ten setts, tending to a nucleus of six movements, in a variety of keys: three in a d-order, three in a D-order, and a chain in a–C–F–B flat.[7] Few sources preserve the selfsame exact sequence in its entirety, or leave internal order unchanged, especially in the d–D setts. Its proximity to the author's intention can be gleaned from the untitled partial sequence surviving in his scorebook. Here he mapped out the later version of the d–D aires only, which gives an authoritative order for the first six setts.

The reason for the rescoring was seemingly solved by Lefkowitz when he uncovered an authentic explanation in a contemporary MS note, by none other than Edward Lowe.[8] Who more respectable than

---

[6] Hayes (1937). See also Campbell, (1975). Ernst Meyer in his pioneering study of the repertoire was inclined to regard the Royall Consort as his 'least sophisticated composition': (1946), 180–3; Erlebach (1932–3), quoting Burney, professed not to 'consider this Consort to be one of his best works; but I hardly think it so bad as Burney describes it'.

[7] Listing as in Dodd, (1980–92). The published ed., Lawes ed. Pinto (1995), reverses nos. 27–8, as listed in Dodd, in the interests of standard order.

[8] GB-Ob, Mus. Sch. MS 236, flyleaf.

Lowe, an academic pillar of Oxford from the 1630s to his death in 1682, and an assiduous copyist of this repertoire? His remarks deserve to be considered just as he formulated them.

> The followinge Royall consort was first composd for
> 2 Trebles a Meane & a Base. but because the Middle
> part could not bee performd with equall advantage to bee
> heard as the trebles were. Therfore the author involved
> the Inner part in two breakinge Bases: which I
> causd to bee transcribd for mee in the Tenor & Counter
> -tenor Bookes belonginge to thes. & soe bound. Wher the
> two breakinge Bases are to be found. & soe many
> figured as agree with thes in Order.

At first sight all is clear, *pace* punctuation. The so-called 'old version' (modern terminology), was devised in the Tr–Tr–T–B–bc (string-quartet) scoring. It then was superseded because of defects inherent in that scoring. Lefkowitz has shown with great clarity how the discarded tenor line was parcelled out between the new bass partnership that paralleled the two treble pair: both of its members took turns to double the basso line while the other descanted in tenor register.

A little reflection leaves room for doubt about the depth of this explanation. As Gordon Dodd remarked, why should it matter if an inner voice in dance-music comes over indistinctly?—unless of course its primary function had been in concert performance, or *Tafelmusik* (as suggested by Peter Holman), which cannot be the whole story.[9] Even more, if this scoring was actively a trammel on presentation of the music, why did it take Lawes so long to twig? Why indeed had he used it in the first place? The old version contains 59 dances, which represents a heavy commitment to an idiom, if it had had problems from the start. Yet it had served other composers well in the preceding decade or longer: Coleman and Jenkins, to look no further. Why was it not good enough for Lawes?

Queries such as these may be resoluble by a closer look at Lowe's selection (for as such it must be regarded), to which his remarks are prefaced: a group of twelve 'flat Ayres' (in *d*) is followed by two more

---

[9] Holman (1993).

37

of 'sharp Ayres' (in *D)* that add a further eleven to make 23. The tenor and countertenor books are now missing, which explains why it has gone unnoticed to date that his selection was taken from the old version. (This can be deduced from the fact that some of the *d–D* aires, including those he copied, underwent a revision for the new version that altered their length: Lowe's are the unrevised lengths.) Lowe may well have later wanted the new bass parts transcribed for him in the missing books; but his primary copies were 'old'. Possibly they represented the hypothesised nucleus of the work rather than a selection from it. It follows that he was not necessarily suggesting an innate superiority in the newer scoring by attempting to speak on the composer's behalf of his intentions. But there is one more factor that still refuses to add up: some surprisingly perfunctory part-writing found in Lawes' wayward tenor part. It spends unusual amounts of its time dogging the bass part at parallel unisons low in its register, or else shadowing the treble lines at the octave below (Ex. 7). It shows disappointingly little team-spirit overall, making scant attempt to fill out harmony or sonority. There may well be some purpose in this, and it is not hard to devise explanations, rather than assume the part to have been a make-weight, a stop-gap introduced to make up team numbers (so to speak) when revamping three-part (Tr–Tr–B) music. One that does occur is that a tenor line with independent counterpoint is a hindrance under practical conditions, especially with dances that are actively choreographed. This affects the corants of the old version more than any other segment; but frequent pause-marks in mid-dance suggest that 'stops' were made in the steps for the performance of extra-musical activities: the 'congees', the waving of kerchiefs, or bestowing of nuts and throwing of sweetmeats that are attested as an English practice. However, for a composer then to make a claim (if it *was* his claim) that the tenor could not be heard to advantage simply will not wash, given that he had never intended a distinct role for it. Said too loudly, comments like that risk application of the old saw, that a bad workman blames his tools. It is increasingly hard to accept this as a full account of the composer's own attitude. Was Lowe then misunderstanding information received, or even actively misrepresenting Lawes?

Ex. 7: Corant (33)

The history of the 'string-quartet' dance-scoring is in itself not straightforward, and its perhaps diverse origins and subsequent uses overlap clear distinctions between chamber music and more public utilitarian ('social') dance, via the *Tafel* (entertainment) function. Much of the background has become clear as distinctions between repertoires and the instruments used to play them have been established. Peter Holman's study of the violin's time-honoured association with the dance sheds light on the evolution of a two-treble scoring as it diverged from the normal Renaissance five-part graded (Tr–A–T–Bar–B) ensemble. Ideally a survey should take into account the previous use of two-treble scoring in both wind and vocal repertoires; but for

39

present purposes it may be taken for granted that opportunity for a general change was ripening by 1600.[10]

As early as John Dowland's collection of five-part pavans, galliards and almans, the famous *Lachrimæ* (1604), a single galliard out of the 21 items printed adopted the two-treble scoring (in replacement of Tr–A). The direction of two-treble style thereafter for the next two decades in England is more difficult to follow. Five-part MS dances in a mixture of the two scorings occur in a collection linked to the Oxford organist William Wigthorpe, *c*.1610 (now GB-Lbl, Add. 17786–91); two pavans apparently written for two trebles by the Dane, Mogens Pedersøn, during his stay in England, 1611–14, occur in MSS connected to the other university.[11] In the English context there is no difficulty in calling this a chamber style: we know all too little of what the city waits for the various great corporations would have played, but this style of music is unlikely to have been amongst it, so early in the century. The Jacobean fantasy repertoire, though, that blossomed in the century's first two decades, was predominantly for five to six instruments in two-treble scoring; even if the most senior of the composers, Ferrabosco II, stuck to the graded ensemble for his five-part pavans, almans and In Nomines. (He, like Orlando Gibbons, seems to have regarded five-part writing as a Tr–A preserve for these forms, distinct from the free-fantasy repertoire.) What is harder to show is how, when or why the slimming-down process, through omission of tenor lines, took place. To an extent dating is clearer from Germany, as pointed out by Holman. There, a taste existed for printed instrumental dance such as never quite caught on in England; and the printed collections contained a large input from expatriate English players (esteemed away from home for their gamba playing), either their own works or arrangements of basic versions cadged from bigger names; all to bring the pleasures of the Tr–Tr–T–B–bc scoring to amateurs keen to sample the inventive masque dances emanating

---

[10] Holman (1993).
[11] Payne (1991), nos. 26–7. Different selections from the dances of Add. 17786–91 were published in Fellowes (1924) and Warlock (1926). Four undistinguished anonymous pavans for the 2Tr 5-part ensemble of much the same date are in GB-Lbl Add. MSS 17792–6: see *SP* 149.

from the English court, by masters like Robert Johnson. Much of this was doubtless rescored for the particular purposes of each publication. The hand of Thomas Simpson, editor of the innovative *Taffel-Consort* (Hamburg, 1621) has been seen as a general arranger of contents in that publication.[12] Certainly some of the dances seem to have been rejigged into an ungrateful scoring (by transposing a tenor line up an octave into Tr II register) that does little to aid clarity or tunefulness; the masque dances as originally performed in public are unlikely to have been clogged with this hindrance to easy acceptability. The place of origin therefore of the two-treble scoring is unclear, perhaps inevitably in a fairly closely-knit world of small courts across Protestant northern Europe, where trends were quickly assimilated. In the English fantasy too, even by 1620, the smaller-scale ensembles began to take advantage of this self-raising mix. Pride of place goes to Orlando Gibbons' innovative published *Fantazies of III. Parts.* (1622), where five of the nine pieces are in Tr–Tr–B scoring (no continuo specified).[13] The four-part fantasy also hankered after this lightness; a shift to the two-treble texture was evident in an influential sequence by Ferrabosco II, which predates 1620, and derivative works by Richard Mico which must be soon after. These vary Tr–A with Tr–Tr texture. Inventive pieces by Lupo in the two-treble scoring for three and four parts colonise the ever-vaguer territory separating contrapuntal fantasy from aire.[14] As a result it becomes harder to see firm dividing lines in the regnal year of 1625, when Charles I succeeded his father James on the throne, and the trends initiated by his personal musicians looked set to breath new life into the status quo of the inherited king's establishment. But the change that was in the air was not restricted to any one clique. As noted by Holman, the musicians at James' funeral numbered Maurice Webster, second-generation expatriate returnee from Germany, recruited from the small court at Bückeburg. Was Webster a catalyst sufficient to bring about the dominance of the string-quartet scoring? This theory seems to create an

---

[12] T. Simpson ed. Thomas (1988).
[13] See Pinto (forthcoming *a*), on dating.
[14] Lupo ed. Charteris and Jennings (1983), nos. 3–13.

unreal importance for a player-composer whose extant dances are unimpressive for quality and quantity; one could argue contrariwise that he was acceptable in England mainly because his German training was close enough to the English pattern to enable him to fit in with stylistic advances made before his employ. Whichever way round the evidence fits, Webster was not the mastermind that conceived of suite-form as found in the Royall Consort and as it set the precedent for the coming age, since this development belongs more closely to a time immediately after 1630 (about 8 years after his advent), and to two other player-composers in particular.

A brief look at the few surviving sources is necessary to see the process at work that led to the Royall Consort. (Those for the old version of the Royall Consort itself, by the way, are surprisingly late and unhelpful here: the two main ones, both in the Music School collection of Oxford University, seem to have been there since their time of copying in the later 1650s and are tardy witnesses to the genesis of the opus.) There had been a period of evolution now partially lost to view, both in scoring and in the business of fitting together *ad hoc* suites from heterogeneous items. The chief composers in the process are John Jenkins and Charles Coleman, preceded to a lesser extent by Robert Johnson II, Maurice Webster and some of the old guard, and followed half a step later by Lawes and Simon Ives. Four of these sources have been discussed by Holman.[15]

First in time come three that began existence in London, the earliest of which has returned there from abroad (GB-Lbl Add. MS 36993), and the other two that survive at Christ Church, Oxford, their home since the 17th century (Mus. 367–70 and 379–81). The basic ingredient in the dance-repertoire of all three is the alman, which had almost totally ousted the pavan as main functional dance by 1630. The four-part set of books, Mus. 367–70, has 52 almans, against nine pavans, nine corants, three sarabands and one galliard. Corants and the few sarabands occur there intermingled, in the random order in which they arrived in the copyists' hands: but then, significantly, the owner of the Christ Church sets added indices to the pieces by key, in order to ease the formation of groups. The alman–corant–saraband

---

[15] Holman (1993).

combination, in which the catalyst seems to have been the saraband, was here possibly being imposed.

Add. 36993 in some respects witnesses an earlier stage, though its contents concord very closely with the other two MSS. It is set out in five key-sequences, entirely of almans, except that all but the last are headed by a pavan. The first of these pavans (in C, by Dering) is the only one linked by composer to the succeeding alman; but all the same the marks are of a striving towards consistent practice.[16] Consistent scoring too is to be seen emerging. Add. 36993 is described (in mid-contents) as a 'Continued Base' partbook. It gives a single line, written in ordinary 'French' tablature as for a lute, but presupposes an instrument at bass-viol pitch which, though a relatively unusual survival, marks a use of tablature for bowed instruments reported as common around 1600, by the lutenist Thomas Robinson.[17]

Headings to the pieces specify either four or five parts; but that does not necessarily confirm that they were performed with the full complement. Because of the precedence given to key-order it may just be the copyist's way of indicating the original scoring, and hence even imply a performance for smaller forces such as the string-quartet form. The two Christ Church sets belonged to a significant collector of the 1630s, John Browne (of whom more below, and in Chapter V), and were commissioned from a professional copyist on whom Browne modelled his own hand when he took over copying.[18] They too show that two-treble scorings in three to four part textures were only just becoming normative at the time of copying, and were preceded by three-part Tr–A–B and four-part Tr–A–T–B ensembles.[19]

Dating of sources is the main key to the emergence of suite-form. John Browne's dance-sets were in all probability compiled in the first half of the 1630s; they preserve in fact the tail-end of a Jacobean dance-repertoire by Ferrabosco II, and lesser lights like Thomas Ford, William

[16] Dodd (1980–92) lists this initial pavan separately as a 4-part anon. work, no. 1315, owing to lack of titling.
[17] Robinson (1603), sig. Cijv: 'by your skill in playing vpon the Lute, and the knowledge you haue in the pricksong, you may verie easilie attaine to play vpon the Viol *de Gambo*, either by *Tabliture* or by pricksong notes.'
[18] Ashbee (1977).
[19] A more extended discussion of this occurs in a concurrent article, Pinto (forthcoming *b*).

Cranford and others, caught before consignment to oblivion. Mention too should be made of John Jenkins, on more than one count. Browne preserved entire his beautiful and well-nigh unique dances for four-part, graded ensemble, Tr–A–T–B, in alman, corant, saraband forms (unordered into setts). No continuo survives for these earlier partbooks, though some extra basso parts are found for the few of these dances that entered collections compiled after the mid-1630s.[20] Browne also had access—not at first hand—to a wide range of the newer string-quartet works by Jenkins, who is a significant developer of the scoring's potential.[21]

Jenkins, however, was a perennial outsider, and regrettably the circumstances under which he worked have been lost to view. The reason for that can be summed up in one phrase: the Fire of London. As noted in the monograph on Jenkins by Andrew Ashbee, there must have been a wide swathe of destruction caused just before 1670 to the property of city families like those where Jenkins was apparently most employed in his earlier years. The incalculable loss of documentary material could well affect our knowledge of many other composers, not least the Lawes brothers.[22] Browne was not apparently close to Lawes either, even if a few of the better-circulated early four-part aires in *g* had come his way. What he does effectively record is the development of another composer who like Lawes moved in from the periphery to the centre of events about 1630: Charles Coleman.

Coleman is a now underregarded figure, who must have featured rather larger in his own times: a major contributor to John Playford's mid-century publications of Tr–B aires, dance-music in two to four parts with continuo forms the bulk of his extant output.[23] His origins like those of Jenkins were in city music rather than the inward-looking foreign families that dominated the circles of the king's private music.[24] From apparently irregular involvement with the

[20] All Tr–A–T–B dances in Jenkins ed. Pinto (1992).
[21] The 2Tr dances are in Jenkins ed. Ashbee (1992 and 1993).
[22] Ashbee (1992), 26 and *passim*.
[23] Fullest listing in Dodd, (1980–92).
[24] Klinkenborg (1981) gives a facsimile (including music) from Robert White's masque *Cupid's Banishment*, enacted at Deptford, 4 May 1617 for Queen Anne, and including the young Coleman amongst its cast. Verbal text reprinted in Nichols (1828), iii. 283–96; the musical text appears to be unstudied.

'Consort', the lutes, viols and voices that performed privately for the king, he made more permanent entry into royal activities by his attachment to the music of the Prince of Wales (the later Charles II, born 1630).[25] In common with Lawes, who whatever his connections and abilities was also no more than up-and-coming until 1635, he is thereby the less likely to have made his contribution to the new dance repertoire directly for court revels; an origin slightly outside that sphere must be sought for their input.

Coleman is also useful for reasons of style. He shows the same

Ex. 8: Alman (257)   Charles Coleman

[25] Ashbee (1988); Holman (1993).

schooling as Jenkins in all but the most intimate and personal gestures. It is instructive to view how close the two are, from comparable almans in Browne's copies—and how large the distance is, in that
undefinable vividness that comes through inimitably in the phraseology of Jenkins (Exx. 8–9). The songbird tunefulness of Jenkins seems
to be echoed by Coleman's native approach to dance-melody; in contrast, the later style of Coleman has more the acquired flavour of the
hocketing canonic trebles in a very trim antiphony that sharply recalls Lawes (see Exx. 10–11). There is no real telling who had priority
in it, and it would be pointless to insist on one, where the important
thing is to recognise that a shared working environment contributed
to the development of both.

Ex. 10a: Alman (79)   Charles Coleman

47

14

19

Ex. 10b: Alman (31)

Ex. 10c: Alman (24)

Ex. 11a: Saraband (80) Charles Coleman

Ex. 11b: Corant (26)

There is no record of other association between the men, and relations could even have been cool. If they had been as close as genre suggests, then one would have expected to see Coleman's name among the elegists paying tribute after Lawes' death. Everything known about Coleman, such as the city links, the acquaintance with prominent puritans like the Hutchinsons, the acceptance of a Cromwellian court post, goes to indicate a very different outlook from that of Lawes. But it can be inferred that Coleman developed towards Lawes by examining a slightly later set of books. GB-Och, 353–6 is a set of three-part dances by Coleman, Tr–Tr–B–bc; it was probably commissioned by John Browne, since his hand filled up a large part of the following blank space with a series of four-part fantasies by Richard Mico.[26] From the fact that some of these pieces by Coleman in the three-part scoring overlap with the four-part repertoire, and from the presence of a continuo book, it is likely that the set dates from a few years later than Browne's previous dance-sets: say 1635–8 (about the time, that is, that John Hutchinson was receiving tuition in Richmond). Browne's music collection, as I have tried to indicate elsewhere, can all be dated before 1642 and the outbreak of war, since most of it ended up in the royalist stronghold of Oxford, which cannot have been to the satisfaction of its Parliamentarian owner-copyist![27]

These three-part books show the process of suite-formation one crucial step ahead of that in Browne's earlier books; they have sequences by key of pavans (or pavan-almans), almans, corants and sarabands with the odd galliard, just as in the setts by Lawes; the opening setts moreover are in the same keys as those that have a high probability of being the nucleus for the Royall Consort as a whole. There is an unmistakable similarity between the pavans or pavan-almans that head these setts in the works of both men, as though written in close conjunction (Exx. 12–13). Other setts in g–G and B

[26] Pinto (forthcoming b). A complete survey of Browne's collection has been so far impractical, despite the large coverage in Ashbee (1977), owing to an attempt elsewhere to attract the credit for the discovery; other items as important as GB-Och 353–6 remain to be discussed. For Mico's works see Mico ed. Hanley (1994) = MB LXV.

[27] Ashbee (1977), Pinto (1978). See too Ch. V below.

Ex. 12a: Pavan (101)   Charles Coleman

Ex. 12b: Pavan (8)

Ex. 13a: Pavan-Alman (71)   Charles Coleman

51

Ex. 13b: Pavan-Alman (29)

flat follow in 353–6, and it is hard to resist a feeling that similar common material is employed here too. Whenever the vogue for alman–
corant–saraband suites reached London from its probable origina-
tors, the lutenists of the Parisian salons just before 1629, these setts
must be among the first attempts in England to adapt it for dance-
ensemble. Ascertainable credit for the advance belongs indistinguish-
ably to Coleman as to Lawes—indeed, from surviving sources there
is nothing to show that Coleman was not there first. The time taken
by his setts to trickle through to Browne cannot be gauged, even if
Browne as a Presbyterian of puritanical upbringing may have had
more direct links with Coleman than other royal musicians; but a
date *c*.1633–6, or even earlier, for the innermost circle to have established suite-form for ensemble writing is far from unreasonable.

   Some things about the Royall Consort's inception are clearer as
a result, taking into account internal features. Most of the pieces in
the *d–D* orders were written first, initially only loosely divided into
setts. Their priority is clear from one point in especial. The dances in
D show the only real sign of rethinking in terms of altering phrase-
lengths, and even that only at cadences, where Lawes took pains when
making out the Tr–Tr–B–B versions to allow all the bowed parts
breathing-space. (This reshaping occurs in nos. 22–3, 25–6, 31, 33.)
The single paven of substance in these setts is no. 8 in *d*, a piece of
inventive variety and original, dashing figuration, that could well
have been intended as a curtain-raiser for the entire order in *d*, before

the addition of fantasy-movements had come to mind. By combining orders from the numerous later partbook copies, it is possible to guess at an ordering: into two sequences of about 18 dances each (three groups of six, perhaps, or two of nine).[28] How next they developed is less certain.

Suggested nucleus of Lawes, Royall Consort sequences

d-order:	8	19	11	9	10	12	13	[14?]	15	16	18	20	21	2	3	4	5	6
	P	A	C	A	A	C	S	[S]	A	A	C	C	S	A	A	C	C	S

D-order:	38	30	26	27	28	22	23	24	25	41	29	37	31	33	32	39	34	35
	A	A	C	S	S	P	A	C	C	M	A	A	A	C	C	C	S	S

The total of differences between the old and new versions for the d–D setts, so far as melodic invention goes, is relatively small. It implies a fairly close time-interval before restructuring. That could well make the decision to rescore these orders one that occurred only shortly before the development of the later setts in a, C, F, B flat, where partbook copies hardly vary internal order at all. In the later setts, the style of partwriting shows shifts of attitude. The trebles' peculiarly tight and metallic caccia-at-all-costs, found in the d–D setts, is replaced by a free-breathing and extended type of antiphonal canon. It is closer in fact to the imitative texture found in the setts for two violins, where the majority of the dances (14 out of 16) do not have block-harmony entries. A dating of somewhere around 1634–6 is a reasonable one for the violin works, on the basis of the circulated copies which must have been available to amateurs by 1638–9: one small sign to suggest that the revised Royall Consort was towards the end, rather than near the beginning, of this period.[29] The tenor parts for these 'later' setts of the Royall Consort announce their entry

[28] See Lawes ed. Pinto (1995), introduction, and critical commentaries for fuller tables displaying source-order.

[29] See Lawes ed. Pinto (1991) nos. 11b, 12b for the non-imitative entries. The opening phrase of no. 11b (in a) seems comparable to Royall Consort no. 45, alman in a. Some other detail is also reminiscent; cf. hocketing in second strains: in no. 16b (in D), bars 23–8 with Royall Consort no. 31, alman in D, bars 8–12. John Browne's copies of the violin setts seem to be datable to c.1636–8: ibid. 116.

in more lordly fashion, delaying on occasion by a bar or two (a sign that the version for bass viol was by now uppermost in the composer's mind). Two set-piece pavans, in F and B flat, make their appearance. In the old version however, which presumably by now was synchronous with the new, there is no sign of the pavans in a and C. Later even than the establishment of parallel old and new versions, one must then assume a further stratum of additions. Alongside the fantasies and 'eccos' stand these two pavans, which possess unusual chordal textures; the reason for which is shown by their aptness as a prerequisite for virtuoso divisions, such as added to the pavan in C in one set of parts.

Why exactly the rescoring (and aggrandisement, by inclusion of the serious pieces, pavans and fantasies, that had not thitherto been considered apt) came about is still mysterious. One can suggest explanations related to performance-practice , such as a move to a larger acoustic, or different function: as concert-music proper, that is, rather than pure wallpaper. One thing is clear: music in a two-treble scoring was not primarily, or ever, intended for performance on the widest scale; as insertion in masque-music, that is, or even as public dance. Perhaps court revels when on an intimate scale would have had a place for them; Lawes did after all rescore one alman (no. 38) 'For the Violins of 2. Trebles', which means the regular violin court ensemble; even so, he maintained the two-treble scoring. You might say that historically both these scorings were destined to fall short of expectations once the circumstances that produced them had evaporated; as to some extent they did. The rapid transition between various functions of practical dance-accompaniment, *Tafelmusik* and concert perfomance argues for a very alert, socially close-knit recipient body of appreciants.

It is more than possible that Edward Lowe got hold of the wrong end of the stick when reporting that Lawes felt dissatisfied with the scoring, *qua* texture. The composer may well of course have cursed fate for lumbering him with a tenor-bound scoring that no longer commanded respect; but plumping for a two-bass texture in its place is just as likely to have arisen from stylistic reasons, the idiosyncrasies of working within the two-treble idiom. To talk of string quartets is after all a bit misleading, since the early Stuart fashion was historically little more than a by-path off the inexorable advancement on the highway to trio-sonata scoring proper. A two-treble style that is, as a genuine partnership of trebles, brought with it its own emphasis on antiphony and balance; but in England this was for long a vocalic type of interchange of ideas, inherited from the madrigal and its antithetical habits of melodic progression (no wonder that 'echo' effects abounded from the later '20s). In this company a tenor was bound to be gooseberry, with no one constant role or partner to cleave to.

No doubt as a result of this logic, the string-quartet seems to have been wellnigh abandoned towards the end of the '30s in favour of Tr–Tr–B–B scoring. The partbooks of Coleman's three-part dances that were acquired by John Browne at this time show how already at the end of the 1630s people were giving up on the 'string-quartet' scoring in favour of that for 'trio-sonata'. In Coleman's case this reflected common limitations: already players were realising the logic behind two-treble scorings and eliminating unnecessary parts. Coleman of course was less part of the charmed circle than Lawes and could perhaps call on fewer players to work up large-scale dances. In the case of a well-connected court composer, as Lawes had now become, the problem was not finding the full complement of players to assist, up to the traditional limits of six (plus continuo), but how effectively to rescore, or otherwise ensure that lower parts respected the balance that had been achieved in the upper lines. Lawes himself attempted setts for Tr–Tr–B–B in c–C, drafted in his scorebook but possibly never finished (organ parts or other continuo do not survive).[30] Jenkins, beginning possibly around the same time, but more likely a little later, in the mid-1640s, wrote a fine extended sequence of 32 dances for Tr–Tr–B–B to the organ (pavans, almans, galliards, including the famous 'Newarke Seidge' that must commemorate the relief of that town and castle, March 1644) and almost incidentally three fantasies; Christopher Simpson, John Hingeston and others whose careers for the most part postdate 1640, followed.[31]

[30] See Lawes ed. Taruskin (1983) and Lawes ed. Nicholson (1985). The edition by Nicholson, though without score, gives an editorial organ part to supplement an at times rather thin string texture; see below, Ch. 5.
[31] See Jenkins ed. Ashbee (1969), nos. 1–32 = MB XXVI; Hingeston ed. Dornenburg (1992), and listings in Dodd (1980–92).

Of course it may be unnecessary to look for deep motives in the shifts of fashion or image that are inflicted periodically by that most narcissistic of activities, the dance, upon its hapless better half, the music. It decreed that in four-part music, from the earlier '30s on, the wretched tenor part played a declining role. By 1640 it was being ousted from textures in general, as the lyra-viol in consort made something of a revival. For all his advocacy of the 'Grave Musick' found in the fantasy repertoire, Thomas Mace, the author of *Musick's Monument*, had also been fond of consorts in two to four parts, accompanied by the 'harpsicon' (or else the lately-invented 'pedal'), of *'Ayrey, Jocond, Lively,* and *Spruce'* music, which presumably was drawn from the chamber dance-repertoire of the 1630s–50s. When discussing provision of instruments, Mace recommended

a *Pair* of *Violins*, to be in Readiness for any *Extraordinary Jolly*, or *Jocund Consort-Occasion*...to which end, It will be *Requisite*, you *Store* your *Press* with a *Pair* of *Lusty Full-Sciz'd Theorboes*, always to strike in with your *Consorts*.

In addition Mace suggested

to make your *Store* more *Amply-Compleat*; add to all *These* 3 *Full-Sciz'd Lyro-Viols*;...Let *Them* be *Lusty, Smart-Speaking Viols*; because, that in *Consort*, they often *Retort* against the *Treble; Imitating*, and often *Standing instead of that Part, viz. a Second Treble*.[32]

He could have been—possibly was—talking of the ensemble needed for the Royall Consort; but a more general change favoured the bass-sized instruments against the tenors. Lyra consorts by Jenkins survive, in the most famous of which, his '5 Bell Consort', also known as 'Lady Katharine Audley's Bells', the alternation of a lyra-viol with a second violin is attested in extant playing parts.[33] Lyra consorts by Lawes for violin, two lyras, theorbo and harpsichord (or some selection from this array of instruments), like others by Jenkins and

---

[32] Mace (1676) 235, 246.
[33] See Jenkins ed. Traficante (1992), where in this most famous of Jenkins' later works, a 2nd treble exists as alternative to the lyra in some lesser sources (see commentary, pp. xxxiv–xxxvi).

Simpson, are known of, although no longer extant.[34] What Lowe in Commonwealth Oxford may have been doing was valiantly keeping the tenor flame alive, by copying what 'string-quartet' repertoire was available, and perhaps even playing it on a whole consort of viols, even if the composer may have intended the upper parts to have been rendered otherwise. One thing that emerges from Anthony Wood's farcical account of his own progress on the violin (which he began by tuning in fourths, before splashing out on lessons from a reputable tutor) is that the music-meetings presided over by Lowe were decorous affairs. Lowe played nothing but the organ; 'a proud man', noted Wood, he 'could not endure any common musician to come to the meeting, much less to play among them'. Violinists would possibly have been shown the door by this upholder of the social order, until the advent of the miraculous Baltzar brought about a change of heart, in 1658.[35]

In an roundabout way the Oxford cultivation of the by then out-moded string-quartet repertoire raises the question of authentic in-strumentation. The term 'treble', almost universally used except in clear contexts like that of the court violin sett, leaves ambiguous how the top parts would have been rendered. All that can be said here is that despite the superior qualities of the violin on the larger dance-floor, whether it had predominance in the original performing circles of small-scale entertainment is uncertain. Lawes and his colleagues would have been proficient on any type of bowed string, which in-cludes the smaller sizes of viol (as the existence of the viol setts seems to show). How long the treble viol was seriously cultivated, for how long it was in decline, is the type of question for which by its nature no all-embracing evidence is likely to turn up. Roger North remem-bered beginning on the treble viol, around 1660 perhaps, before gradu-ating to the bass. (His grandfather Dudley, brought up before 1612 at the court of the early-deceased Prince of Wales, Henry Frederick, had stuck with the treble viol, never came up to date, and encouraged his children to follow his example.)[36] Some evidence for the use of a pro-totype *pardessus de viole*, specifically for allowing a royal amateur to

---

[34] Traficante (1978–9), 20–22, items ii, iv–vi.
[35] Holman, (1984).
[36] North ed. Wilson (1959), 10.

play treble lines without undue exertion, has turned up for the later 1660s, in Madrid among Spanish royalty; Don Juan of Austria, natural son of Philip IV no less.[37] This must, however, have been an abnormal departure; there is every reason to think that a considerable technical facility existed earlier amongst English treble violists, to judge from from the repertoire played.[38]

The Royall Consort collection is on the large side for a résumé of its excellencies. The growls of Burney have right up to the present day deterred a full appreciation, to an extent that even those who have taken trouble to assess its contents at first hand, like Erlebach and Meyer, have felt inhibited from describing it as quite of the first water, as serious chamber music. The source of Burney's irritation can be pinpointed, at least in part, from his slighting reference to Henry's 'psalmodic' language. Truth is that the age was a formative one in the hymnody of the Anglican rite; literary associates of the Lawes brothers were contributors to the attempts at escaping from the dull churn of Sternhold and Hopkins, and include many sophisticates like Thomas Carew, Henry King—and of course George Sandys, a minor talent but socially well-connected in the 'Arminian', broad-church movement, and one who was set by both Lawes brothers. Psalm-setting was for them more than a perfunctory nod towards obligatory religious duties, and more a way of establishing a set of central and unpuritanical Anglican values. Musical attempts to divest the Genevan straitjacket, the plodding but well-loved tunes like Old Hundredth, were correspondingly made by serious composers—or so   and Henry Lawes deserve to be called, even if their Tr–B harmonisations look lightweight on the printed page. One thing their language did succeed in doing was in influencing the revived 19th-century corpus of hymnody, so that even today the elegance of their ideas of congregational melody has some resonance.

The resemblances go further than that. One can see a likeness, for example, between the opening of a masque dance by William (no.

---

[37] Woodfield (1985) John Aubrey knew of Philip IV himself as a devoted tenor-violist.

[38] Coates and Dart (1955) = *MB* IX no. 95 transcribes 'A Devision for a trible violl to play wth a virginall', based on the popular tune 'Barafostus' Dream': GB-Lbl Add. MS 36661, f. 57r–v.

209) with the contour of the well-loved hymn *Repton*, 'Dear lord and father of mankind', as arranged from Parry's oratorio, *Judith*.[39] Similarities to hymnody should not be brushed away, and one must conclude that it is part of the unfinished business that even now is inherited from this era. Hence in some part the way that the deliberately limited contours to the suave public melody of the age strike us as playful, almost toylike, as found in the Royall Consort and elsewhere (the viol consorts are a slightly different kettle of fish, but the same sort of melodic invention is found in them too). Feelings about decorum influence responses to scale as well as tunefulness. One feels almost obliged to make allowances for trivial dances, churned out by the square footage. The opus, though, was always more than that, and overflowed its composer's intentions to such an extent that the spillage resulted in the magnificent large-scale pavans and fantasies, the imposing triumphal arches that lead one into the smaller-scale domestic ménage.

The priority of the *d–D* orders, two violin keys typical of entertainment and masque, is perhaps because they bring to mind the twin public qualities of kingship, that of majestic force held in reserve against wrongdoers, and of equally godlike bounty for the deserving. One finds the customary gambits to capture attention, like almans headed with the 'narrative' rhythmic formula (nos. 2–3, and variations thereon in 19 and 30). Lawes of course drew on a stock of habitual motifs and procedures; it is instructive to compare a published dance from Playford's *Court-Ayres* (1655), no. 137 (Dodd aire no. 233), with similar ideas in Royall Consort aire no. 19—here lateness of publication does not of course prove lateness in composition (Ex. 14a–b). The shape of the second strain contributed towards the subsequent five-part viol-consort aire in *c* (no. 77) discussed below in Chapter 3. Lawes specialised in smooth walking basses perhaps more than any other composer of the time. Above it he imposed the two-treble duet, in a whirling dialogue of great rhythmic force and canonic insistence (cf. 3, 6, 15–16, 20, 23–4, 26, 37). This bass can march up (20), down

---

[39] This aire is the 'Valediction' from Davenant's *Britannia Triumphans* (1638), and occurs in GB-Ob MS Mus. Sch.B.2, p. 17 in a 3-part(Tr–T–B) version. See Lawes ed. Lefkowitz (1970) for a reconstruction of the incidental music.

Ex. 14a: Alman (233)

Ex. 14b: Alman (19)

(2–3, 19) or, Duke of York-fashion, one after the other (32). The 'Ecco' pieces (7, 40) are from their phrasing presumably stylised corants; they begin on repeated high a" calls, in Lawes' typical corant fashion (cf. 5, 12, 17–18, 39, 40, 58, 61; similar high g" is prominent in the dances in C, and e" in the sett in a).

Dances are of course repeated *ad libitum* to the satisfaction of the dancers, and there is no sustainable logical divide between basic written versions and extemporised, decorated versions, or even the repetition forms that emerge from basic dance patterns. All these, since the time of the early Renaissance *basse-danse*, had customarily been founded on bass *ostinati*. It is worth noting though that at only one point does Lawes attempt through-composed repetition form: in

60

saraband no. 21, where a six-bar ground-bass is repeated four times. Lawes called the piece a saraband, but there is little of the lilting dotted rhythms that normally give this dance its sparkle, and the use of thematic material is tightly controlled through interchange between the parts. The bass has an appreciable though not exact resemblance to the *folia* pattern ('Les Folies d'Espagne', most familiar from its later-century title as 'Farinell's Ground'). The closest resemblance to the *folia* is found in the saraband of the first sett in *d*, piece no. 6; a distinct general similarity to the same bass pattern also infects the two sarabands of the second sett, nos. 13–14 (see Ex. 15). These last two show,

Ex. 15: Saraband in *d*

rather than deviations on the route to establishment of this famous variation bass in its later-17th-century form, signs of proximity to preceding extemporised patterns; far from negligible as evidence of the saraband's shape at a relatively early stage in England.[40] It is also supplementary indication that all these sarabands in *d* (including the one that by chance has not survived in the old version, no. 14) were part of Lawes' initial design for the 'royall' *ordres*, since the sarabands of the setts deemed here to be later have moved further away from such stock basses. In the old version of the saraband no. 21, if not the new, an eightfold repeat of the six-bar pattern may be called for, since the tenor part occurs in two complementary versions that imply a double gallop through.

Perhaps the least enthralling dances are the pavans. Some of them are more accurately designated pavan-almans. Recognisable from a binary (two-strain) form, a pavan-like harmonic flow, but with incidental rhythmic detail more typical of an alman, and tending to be shorter than 30 bars, the pavan-alman was certainly recognised as a distinct cross-breed in this time. Playford's dance-publications include some, so-named, by John Carwarden and Charles Coleman, in *Court-Ayres*.[41] There is no lack of earlier Stuart dances that seem to fall into an intermediate group: Alfonso Ferrabosco II, five-part 'Pavan' no. 9, which for lyra-viol occurs in his *Lessons* (1609), no. 8; and Jenkins, four-part aires no. 49, 'Ayre' (this last in ternary form, but no pavan). The instance by Lawes, no. 29, begins promisingly with one of his specialities, repeated in strain two: unison sonority shared by

[40] See also Ex. 4b for a similar harmonic pattern. Aire no. 264, a saraband ascribed to Lawes on the basis of one source out of 8 otherwise unattributed, is also comparable (printed in Lawes ed. Pinto (1995) old version). R. Hudson (1982) discusses old and new patterns in the *folia*, said to have reached its high-baroque form around 1670. H. Butler ed. Phillips (1991) contains versions of the *folia* by this expatriate Englishman working in Spain and elsewhere.
[41] Playford (1655) nos. 174, and 120, 127 for Carwarden and Coleman. See also GB-Ob. Mus. Sch. E.410–14 for Coleman, aires 71 in *D* (a4), 191 in *F* (a3); Brewer no. 2 in *c* in Mus.Sch. E.431–6 and GB-Lbl Add. 31429; also Hingeston's 3-part sett for Tr–T–B no. 6 in *a* , and his 5 part sett no. 2 a5 in *g* for a 3-strain piece, all under this title. These last pieces seem to belong to the 1650s; an earlier sett *c*.1640 is that by George Hudson for a lyra-viol consort, beginning with a pavan-alman followed by a straight alman; see G. Hudson ed. Stoltzfus (1981).

the trebles that thereafter breaks down into antiphony. Rather than a rhythmically counterpoised unison, it is one of bright sheer immobility. Somehow though the little quaver imitated figures of the second part lack conviction, through their too-close resemblance to ideas already dealt with in strain one; and the figuration recalls, without matching in effectiveness, the balance between the strains and the harmonic variation in the other pavan-alman in D, no. 22, (if pavan-alman it can be called in this case, being a ternary dance). No. 22 executes a well-judged brief tumble into c sharp minor before its last falling phrases.

Lawes wrote few real pavans: partly because they were outmoded for practical use, of course; partly because he was least happy where obliged to wallow in an undynamic sonority without a forward impetus to its goal, as the reflective nature of the abstract pavan required. And so the Royall Consort's original pavans, no. 8 in d, possibly nos. 55 and 62 in F and B flat too (though the last of these could fall into a pavan-alman mould), require some explaining. The inventive figuration of the paven in d, and its parallels in Coleman, seem to single it out as the original entry dance for the Royall Consort as a whole. That in F offers the shortest way in to Lawes' intention for the remainder, by its resemblance to the chamber pavan as it had ended up in the late 1620s, in the hands of Henrietta Maria's English musicians: the two Richards, Dering and Mico. Dering's pavan–alman pair is found in a single surviving partbook, GB-Lbl, Add. 36993; also in the partbooks of the voracious amateur Sir Nicholas L'Estrange (GB-Lcm 1145), copied at much the same time and an indispensable source for almost all Dering's dance-couples. These two pieces also occur separately, in different sets belonging to Browne. Mico's five-part pavans (solitary works that form their own sequence, since no almans were composed, or else they do not survive) circulated more widely amongst amateurs than Dering's, but seem to take their inspiration from him.

Though it has been assumed that all of Mico's chamber music dates from his earlier days as an Essex household musician, there is no real evidence for this outside the music itself. Probabilities point a slightly different way. In the context of the evolving dance-repertoire, the transition to four-part writing of the string-quartet type shown in

Mico's work (to a lesser extent in Dering) confirms that it is near in time to the transition to suite-form found in Coleman and Lawes.[42] Mico received wages as a successor of Dering in the Queen's Music from 1630. It is however almost inconceivable that this was a fresh appointment without prior knowledge of the establishment; one must presume a few years of steady deputising beforehand. If it is still unclear whereabouts in the previous decade to fit the dances in four to five parts by Mico (close to Dering's), it does not diminish by far the likelihood of their general availability as a model in the 1630s.

In some ways of organisation Lawes shows the impact of these late pavans: their odd combination of periods of stasis, often chromatic or richly discordant, with others of rapid movement. That pattern explains the opening of the pavan in F: a basic harmonic scheme of tonic–dominant, over which washes the chordal ebb and flow of an indistinct alternation between 3–4–3 positions. On the question of nomenclature, one regrets the composer's (and subsequent copyist's) sloth in not bothering to give explicit titles to many of these dances beyond 'aire' *tout court*; if the intention was specific enough at the time of composition (or point of first consumption), it quickly becomes less clear. Even contemporary copyists had occasional difficulty in deciding whether a piece was a corant rather than a saraband; which strengthens the impression that to some extent pieces were neutral hangers on which to fit differing dance-steps and speeds. There is only one galliard to be found in the totality of the Royall Consort, unnamed but identifiable by old-style white notation. Many of the corants, however, like this single galliard, have points of comparison to the galliard-type aires that Lawes, following faithfully the model of Coprario, included in the two-violin setts; these insistently gnaw at the rhythmic bones of repeated-note motifs, over the bass activities.

If accepted that the switch in scoring took place in mid-stream of composition, it does not necessarily mean that the two distinct sections into which the final Royall Consort falls were composed conjunctly. The first and longer part could have accumulated

[42] Sources for the 4-part pavans are restricted to the presumed autograph GB-Lcm 1197, and a set in the hand of a copyist connected to court music, GB-Lms (now housed at Lbl), Mad. Soc. G.33–6. They may not therefore long predate the mid-'30s.

64

piecemeal over the earlier 1630s, until it was eventually rescored. One would like to accept the composer's score of the d–D setts as a final version; but it is a whit disconcerting to find that the partbook copies of the 'new' sometimes agree with the 'old' in some small features against this autograph score. Quite possibly something not totally polished had gone into circulation before Lawes got round to the intended final draft. The place where contents and order show most signs of collage is in the last sett he added to the score, the 8th (in D). Much as happened in Lawes' other big scorebook when the later setts for viols were inserted, they were fitted round the edges of previously filled sections. Right at the end of the Royall Consort mass as copied, and as in the present standard order, come (pp. 95 ff.) the second alman of the 6th sett (38), fantazy (36) and morris (41); the two others now grouped with them, alman (37) and corant (39), were fitted in on a blank folio (pp. 48–9) just before the start of the Royall Consort section on p. 50, which begins with the fantasy in d (1). Since it is the stunning fantasies in d–D and pavans in a and C that the late partbooks tend not to copy, there is justification for seeing these four pieces in particular as Lawes' finishing touches, keystones giving permanence to the subordinate voussoirs. These last-named pavans do not, in common with the whole of the setts they come from, survive in autograph form. There is only one partbook source extant to transmit a version of the piece that offers some of the most florid and extraordinary moments in Lawes' output: the division sections which transfigure the Pavan in C, where the fairly intricate texture is comparable to those of the two fantasy movements in rising to six real parts.

It begins modestly enough with only four real voices in strain 1a; 1b effects interchange of violins, giving violin 2 the chance to flower in variation divisions on violin 1 material. Hereupon the theorbo (bc) line is handed over to unison bass viols, while theorbos are permitted their own free divisions on the bass material. Similar inversions diversify strain 2b; violin 2, which is defective in the sole copy of the strain, presumably borrowed violin 1's line from 2a, since violin 1 in 2b plays a dividing version of violin 2's line from that previous (unvaried) first run. Strain 2b is also the basses' turn to divide, and theorbos here stick to their own unadorned line. In 3b, violins 1 and

2 once more interchange; bass viols take over the continuo line. The theorbos share the previous bass-lines between them. This time the divisions are a free-for-all, beginning with theorbos (bars 60–3), then basses (62–5), then violins, while the four underparts briefly join forces on the single basso line (66–8). After this the texture is shot through with rapid interchange of divisions between violins and viols (69–72) and a final four bars of total dividing in all parts.

The interdependence of the pairs of like instruments, as well as of each strand with the others, is a notable feature of the plan. Writing of this brilliance may well take its departure from casual divisions founded on a well-laid prior scheme, but moves well beyond mere extemporisation as written-out divisions tend to do. It gives grounds for supposing that the pavan in *a*, laid out (most unusually for Lawes) in a similar even minim gait, with ample uniform chordal phrasing, was also planned as a launchpad for divisions on this level. If so, they regrettably were never written down, to our knowledge; though an adventurous performing group could (perhaps should) supply some. The pavan in C thereby occupies a quite unique place in English 17th-century repertoire, for pervasive division-work; it may lack the playful variety injected by tripla episodes into the 'Harpe Consort' works, but this is due to the scale of the project. For six-part writing comparable in any way one has to look back to Peter Phillips' Passamezzo Pavan, highly atypical for England in being a variation form on a Renaissance ground written for six-part ensemble, and for that reason possibly imported back from Phillips' Continental exile. Also comparable are the wellnigh unique variations by Orlando Gibbons on 'Goe from my window': both pieces by Phillips and Gibbons are built on standard bass patterns.[43]

The set of partbooks which is the sole source for Gibbons' piece has been supposed to date from the civil-war period and the wartime court at Oxford itself, since the commissioner of them, Sir

[43] Phillips ed. Coates and Dart = *MB* IX, no.90; Gibbons ed. Harper (1982)=*MB* XLVIII, no. 40. Ibid. nos. 41–2 are Gibbons' 6-part P–G pair, linked to 'Goe from my window' by key and apparently by opening motto of the pavan. A 5-part variation set attributable to William Cranford exists on the same folk-tune; see Dodd (1980–92). The only other 6-part P–G pairs of the period are those by Byrd and Tomkins.

Christopher Hatton III, was comptroller of the royal household there until the fall of Oxford in 1646, and the copyists may have been resident there also, as his household staff. It would be pleasant to think of Oxford in warfare as a nest of singing-birds (the reputation acquired by the Foreign Office, during the time of Austin Dobson); but much about this theory is suppositious and rests on unsubstantiated beliefs about what music-making will have been possible in the very restricted conditions of a garrison city.[44] Of course the beauty of the Royall Consort is the relative economy of scale, the relative mobility of the playing group required (even bass viols can be strapped round the neck at a pinch) and the large musical return on this modest investment. The implication would be then that the pavans in *a* and C had not been thought out before autumn 1642 at the earliest, the date of the king's pitching on Oxford as a headquarters. It is a distinct possibility; but signs are that the main work of establishing the scope of the revised version dates from a little before that.

The overriding characteristic of the Royall Consort dances as a whole, if one takes them on their ambivalent face-value, as either dance-repertoire, or as listener's music on the level which the waltzes of Strauss have attained for present-day European bourgeoisie, is the consummate smoothness and strength combined of the two-treble duet. Disjunct melodic features there are aplenty (though fewer in the milder keys of *D*, *F* and *B* flat). Unsettling tonal juxtapositions and key-centres are mingled in, but in flatter relief than in the complex viol consorts. What is not present even in the bolder of the 'Royall' fantasy movements is an attempt to reach into the complicated interior landscape, the key-replete range of jostling emotions revealed in the soul-baring esoteric works, to which we are now turning. Instead they offer hard initial motifs whose cuffs have been carefully laundered to show predominantly unruffled conjunct movement, to mitigate the gestures of a more heroic size. The sections that follow are

---

[44] See Willetts (1992) for the most recent reassessment; though the evidence for dating contains an element of circularity. For music attestably performed at wartime Oxford, see Pinto (forthcoming *c*).

well-defined and reliant on a constant motion, or even in the use of sequential rhythm, in the building-up of unambiguous phrase-sequences. The result, for better or worse, lacks the intense momentum of the inner chamber works.

It is hard to tell whether this is an honest public direction in which Lawes was turning himself after the discontinuous textures that punctuate his more personal consort experiments, or whether he himself would mentally have pigeon-holed it as a blander version of the consort experience for more casual listeners. One would hope the former; but anyhow the insistent marching and striving of the fantasy in *d*, in particular, have a piercing rhythmic insistence, perhaps surpassing the best of Lawes' previous output. The deceptive gentleness of the fantasy in *D* (no. 36) sharply differentiates it. After a central chromatic passage very similar to that in his five-part fantasy in *C* for the viols, it blossoms, via an unusual straightforward inserted alman-strain, into a wide arpeggiated phrase. Intensely perfumed above by g sharps, this ushers the theorbos down to their lowest note (AA), and up again in wide jumps that at greatest, an interval of a 16th, equal exactly those of the remarkable six-part aire in *g*. Such a similarity cannot be chance; nor can the contrast in achieved effect. In these two minor-major moods no *angst* or indecision is felt, but the operation of an alert, serene intelligence.

Possibly Lawes was, at the last (which we anticipate here), seeing a way forward to public expression of battened emotions: harmonising the underlying stress engendered by the attempt under Charles I, and his decade of personal rule after 1629, to ensure for the garden of England a repose untroubled by the religious wars of the Continent. It was of course a decade of illusory calm for the well-to-do, as after-events were to prove. Court poets quite consciously glorified England's beneficent autocracy and urged disengagement from wider affairs; the music of the Royall Consort at its grandest parallels this parade of superior wisdom, in a manner not unlike the now almost totally lost masque music that displayed the court's lustre for the world to admire. The words of Thomas Carew, responding to an invitation from his friend Aurelian Townshend to pen elegiac poetry in praise of the achievements of Sweden's Gustavus Adolphus, recently fallen in battle, are well known in literary contexts; they have resonance for court music as well. In declining gracefully, and advising Aurelian to restrict his flight to rural tunes, Carew was too subtle a poet not to go some way to fulfilling the request; but his words have rightly been seen as a partial renunciation of duty, and the temptation to quote from the peroration yet once more is irresistible.

> Tourneyes, Masques, Theaters, better become
> Our *Halcyon* days; what though the German Drum
> Bellow for freedome and revenge, the noyse
> Concernes not us, nor should divert our joyes;
> Nor ought the thunder of their Carabins
> Drowne the sweet Ayres of our tun'd Violins. ...

III
The Five-part Setts

Who were fantasies written for? How do you 'read' a fantasy? If these are the right questions, and if they ever yielded obvious answers, then three centuries have effectively hidden them. The usual assumption, that fantasy music is for the enjoyment of its players only, comes naturally enough in the absence of detailed contemporary accounts provided by 'concert-goers'. Yet concerts in all but name there were, under the contemporary description of 'music-meeting'. Roger North distinguished aptly when he wrote of the novelty of *public* music-meetings, 40 years after Lawes' consort setts were first played. Christopher Simpson, writing in 1667, regretted the changing fashions:

> This kind of music (the more is the pity) is now much neglected by reason of the scarcity of *Auditors* that understand it, their ears being better acquainted and more delighted with light and airy music

(my italics). He thought in terms of the music's reception by an audience without mentioning the purely recreational function for the exercise of the players that (on almost as little evidence) is nowadays assumed to have been the be-all and end-all of the music.[1]

One revealing account of performance occurs in the Jestbook of Sir Nicholas L'Estrange, a devoted copyist and collector of the repertoire, who employed Jenkins as a household musician from time to time, incidentally reaping the benefit of his sense of humour. The story acquired from Jenkins was of a dedicated violist (non-professional, probably), performing in 'a meeting of Fancy Musick, only for the viols and Organ', who interrupted the proceedings to scold some chattering gentlewomen in the audience with the reproof that the music was 'not Vocall, for ... these things were never made for words'.[2]

---

[1] C.Simpson (1667).
[2] GB-Lbl Harleian MS 6395, no. 536; reproduction in Willetts (1961), and repr. in Pinto (1994), Ashbee (1992), 86 n. 156.

Other small remarks reveal that chamber-music affairs bored some listeners just as thoroughly in their day as, with changing repertoires, they have continued to ever since. Roger North , talking about the old In Nomine style at which he enjoyed poking a little fun, commented how the pieces

made a confusion of slow Hush, of wch litle was to be understood. and as I haue bin told, one of my owne family, a lady, at hearing it, & being ask't how she liked it, say^d, she could hear No Musick for the Instruments.[3]

The tale just mentioned, recorded by L'Estrange, shows that a repertoire with its own performing tradition and devoted followers had sprung up by the end of the 1630s; but in the pun on 'vocal' music it betrays a surprising oblivion of the very madrigalian origin, only a generation before, of a sizeable portion of the fantasy literature. Lawes' master Coprario is the most notable example of a writer who seems to have turned his large corpus of five-part Italian madrigals into instrumental fantasies by little more than omission of the text (though that must be far from the whole story).[4] The brief fashion for Italian madrigal and its English imitations had faltered by 1612, at the point when instrumental fantasy gained ground, doing so by ingesting a madrigalian approach to structure and content. The meeting-point of the two may be illustrated by an occurrence in a contemporary poetic manuscript of an English madrigal text: 'How great delight' from the *Songs* a3–6 by Thomas Tomkins (1622), no. 5 a3. An adaptation of Battista Guarini's 'Con che soavità', as famously set by Monteverdi in his *Libro VII* a5 (1619), GB-Ob, MS Rawl. poet. 199 gives a variant on it: 'How great delight breed those sweet lips I tast'. This MS anthology entitles the piece 'A ffancy', as if to mark the link between the Italian *concetto*, the conceptual nub of the lyric, and the musical amplification of it in a polyphonically contrasting sequence of contrapuntally worked 'points'.

---

[3] GB-Lbl, Add. MS 35232, f. 10, early version of *The Musicall Gramarian*.
[4] See Coprario ed. Charteris (1981) for texts. No reconstructions have yet been made from these untexted works, though some possible texts have been suggested: see esp. Charteris (1976), Pinto (1981), Wess (1986).

Coprario is not actually the best example to turn to when trying to view the transition in progress. Other composers like Thomas Lupo and John Ward left fantasies with Italian 'titles', varying in their capacity to perplex since some are obvious incipits for missing poetic texts. Some other titles have no known text to latch onto, and are likely to be freestanding imitations never intended for words. An example of the first type (almost the only one actually reconstructed hitherto) comes in Lupo's five-part 'Ardo', which can be resuscitated as a double text: Guarini's 'Ardo, sì, ma non t'amo', and a *risposta* by his rival Torquato Tasso, 'Ardi et gela à tua voglia'.[5] The chilly logic to this 'conceit' (which rather justifies Coleridge's suspicions of the metaphysicals for twisting iron pokers into true-love knots) explores the ambiguity of 'burning' as a sign of infatuation, the rejected lover alleging that this fire was never of love but contempt. The important thing of course is the peg this gives on which to hang musical contrasts: of speed and repose, euphony and dissonance, counterpoint and homophony. But rather even than reading a fantasy as a metaphysical exercise in logic-chopping, one may need to respect a voice that it is tempting to shut one's ears to: that garrulous Ancient Mariner of a provincial teacher, Thomas Mace of Cambridge. Publishing in 1676 partly in order to make a memorial of traditions that were being swept away, he recorded his enthusiasm for the

Grave Musick. , *Fancies* of 3, 4, 5, and 6 *Parts* to the *Organ*; Interpos'd (now and then) with some *Pavins, Allmaines, Solemn, and Sweet Delightful Ayres*; all which were (as it were) so many *Pathettical Stories, Rhetorical, and Sublime Discourses; Subtil, and Accute Argumentations..*'[6]

This excerpt from a well-known passage is worth repeating just in order to ask if, as well as considering fantasies as 'argumentations' (as from the 'conceits' of madrigal texts there is evidence), there are

[5] Lupo ed. Pinto (1990), no. 19. For a compendium of all other known printed versions setting the same texts see Schuetze (1990). John Ward's 'Cor mio' a5 has been resurrected from the version that circulated as a wordless fantasy: J.Ward ed. Payne (1988) ; though, oddly, the only known score for the piece surviving with verbal text in the bass part has been ignored for the edition. See Pinto (1981, 1994).
[6] Mace (1676), 234.

grounds for thinking of them as 'pathetical stories' (i.e. with a narrative or even programmatic element), and 'sublime discourses' (if not sermons, then anthem-equivalents). It is the scale of the fantasy as it blossomed in the 1630s, under the hands of Jenkins and Lawes, that tempts one to take Mace *à la lettre*; and though the madrigal influence is uppermost in the repertoire by Jacobean times, there is some input from the sacred traditions in domestic vocal music.[7] It is not without relevance to Lawes: in his six-part works, as well of course as re-use of the 'In Nomine' *cantus firmus*, a sacred theme is found reworked (in this case, from one of Lawes' own three-part psalm-settings; see Chapter IV below). A five-part alman, no. 77, was part of an anthem by Henry Lawes; though which was the first use, which the adaptation, is debatable. The exact principles of organisation in fantasies, however, are unknown and, without more explicit contemporary guide than we have, perhaps not strictly speaking recoverable.

Another insight to be borne in mind was the comparison made with the graphic organisation of genre painting, by the lawyer and antiquarian Roger North: a late writer (born 1651), he was nonetheless a pupil of Jenkins' old age, and sympathetic to the values of this outmoded music. In a discussion of musical composition (based, inevitably, upon Horace's *De Arte Poetica*), he recommended musicians to have 'some reall designe' in mind, a painterly one that is, framed to the nature of the subject—the one that he mentioned was a sombre work of Raphael, but there is no reason to think that the new genre of landscape could not also have occurred as a parallel.[8] For North, it seems, a serious musical composition, be it sonata (as with his revered Corelli) or older fantasy, should at best embody the narrative elements contained in high art, in a statically presented but dynamically structured whole; an idea that anticipates the later one of music as frozen architecture. Between Mace and North we have fairly secure ground on which to erect the mental framework for the reception of fantasy music, as it evolved in a continuous tradition, and in

---

[7] Pinto (1981) notes some equivalences: Jenkins, Fantasy no. 4 a5 seems to take its monothematic subject from a setting of 'O lord, in thee is all my trust' a5, ascribed to Orlando Gibbons; a famous 'Dorick' fantasy by John Bull was contrariwise adapted into a 4-part sacred song, 'Fraile man, despise the pleasures of this life'.

[8] North ed. Wilson (1959), 115–23.

the hands of the masters that they mention with approbation; in fact all the best-known figures of the 17th century from Alfonso Ferrabosco II to Matthew Locke. (Mace includes 'one *Monteverde, a Famous Italian Author'* in his list, as an example of others from Italy he does not name who excelled in the fantasy genre; a clear if confused sign of the fantasy's wordless madrigal heritage).[9]

Consort Setts I–II

The blueprint showing how (if not why) Lawes assembled his setts for the viols is happily clear from the first of the autograph scorebooks where he wrote his interim drafts; interim, if only because there is no sign that they were ever intended as the finished article, but rather as the ladder that one scales before pushing it away. (The essential organ part, for a start, is absent.) The early pair of fantasies in *g*, already discussed in Chapter I, were scored in revised form, then a pair in *a* added. The prevalence of fantasy-pairs throughout the repertoire, as betrayed by linked thematic material, leads one to suspect some factor or other in normal conditions that encouraged their formation. Perhaps it was no more than the process of circulation to the music-meetings; in the case of a single piece, production of a set of parts each written on a bifolium for purposes of folding to protect the copying would cry out for use to be made of the spare blank inner page. At this point Lawes decided to add two aires, which complete the first two setts. The fantasy–alman linkages were obviously a second thought, betrayed by the different key-signature for the alman in *g:* two flats, compared to the more normal one flat as found in the fantasy movements. (Current numeration of the five-part works runs 68–83, divided into setts as follows: *g* 68–70; *a* 71–3; *c* 74–7; *F* 78–80; *C* 81–3.)

Strangely enough, in the wellnigh 30 years or so of the Stuart fantasy preceding, there had been no overt move to incorporate fantasies into a sett-form, except in special circumstances. Coprario's 'fantasia-suites' for violins had linked a fantasy with two following

---

[9] Mace (1626), 234.

dances (alman–galliard), a novelty of the earlier 1620s at court, though possibly related to his foreign travels in Germany where suite-forms were better liked. But dances for five to six viols are few, and only the engagingly dotty Martin Peerson at St Pauls attempted to marry some skittishly trivial almans to bathetic fantasies, compatible by little more than identical key. Even the older pavan–galliard couples, at least those thematically linked, are rarer than one might expect. Pavan–alman pairs are also few; here Richard Dering (d.1630) provided a significant model, which could be explained by his participation in court music as organist to Queen Henrietta Maria, Charles' consort.[10] It is not, however, a flourishing background; and expanding on it was perhaps not a firm intention when Lawes added the aire-almans in *g* and *a*.

Almost all of the aires in his five-part setts exist in smaller-scale versions, from the Shirley Partbook examples on, which gives a clear impression of expanding plans. That in *g* (no. 70) dates back to the early sequence in *g*–*G* found associated with the Royall Consort, where likewise occur the two (pavan and alman) scored into F for viols. These earlier had been copied in *G*, probably for the sake of the violins and their open d' string. The aire in *a* (no. 73) had also had a busy former career, in the related key of *g*. Its strangest duty was in serving as base for a song-setting, which surfaced late (in 1678), attributed to Henry Lawes: 'Corinna false! it cannot be' (Ex. 15a).[11] This may of course be a bastardisation of an evidently popular aire, except that the feeble words do seem to date from the 1630s, and may have been contemporaneous with the tune, which served as well for keyboard and solo lyra viol (Ex. 15b). Compared with the consort version it shows how adept Lawes was at spinning out for two trebles the possibilities inherent in a 'single' tune.

---

[10] One can also compare an unusual P–A pair by Thomas Tomkins in F, extant in both 4 parts (Tr–A–T–B) and 5 (reworked, with additional Bar): see Tomkins ed. Irving (1991) = *MB* LIX.

[11] Banister and Low (1678), 68–74. The compilers had access to William's autograph songbook, now GB-Lbl, Add. MS 31432, since they printed some settings otherwise unique to it. GB-Ob Ashmole MS 47, ff. 71v–73 contains the anthology version of the poem; see Pinto (1981). Ex. 15b from US-NYp, Drexel MS 5612, pp. 154–5, no. [114].

Ex. 15b: Mʳ Lawes flat tune

There may be a clue here to the alternation *g–a* in Lawes, since by this time the key-system had begun to exhibit the degrees of feeling found later in the century in Purcell's time, when *g* was associated with doom and death, including the erotic 'death' found especially in pastoral settings.[12] The key of *a* seems to be charged for Lawes with alternate amatory languor and passion, and so the song-version of the attached alman is not after all such an odd re-use. As elsewhere

---

[12] See Price (1984) for key in Purcell.

there is almost a preludial character to the first of these *a* fantasies, a gathering of pent forces to be let free later. Its opening still shows the influence of Coprario, in being a 'double fuge' on the lines he advocated in his treatise on composing.[13] The amatory context of the key is comparable to one of Coprario's own borrowings, the head-motif for his four-part fantasy, no. 2 (Ex. 16), which he reworked from a four-part canzonet by Hans Leo Hassler, 'Io son ferito, Amore'.[14] The theme devised by Lawes is not indebted except in the widest sense to

Ex. 16: Fantasy no. 2 a4   John Coprario

Ex. 17: Fantasy (71)

the shape of Coprario's borrowing, but obviously grows out of the tension between the minor sixth and the fifth of the scale, in a similar way (Ex. 17). A continuo-like scale-segment in the bass combines with and develops naturally into a sweeping melody first heard in Tenor I above it (Tenor II in bars 12–16 runs the two together). For a composer

[13] Coprario (*c*1610), ff. 39v–40.
[14] Hassler (1590), no. ix.

78

who as been adjudged 'unlyrical'—in his songs, that is—it is a singularly fluid and extended flight of tune; unusual too, for an opening 'point', in passing through opposed chromatic inflexions on the 6th–7th degrees of the minor scale. The opportunity this leads to for dissonance is not refused. The intent of the contrapuntal movement of parts is still nominally orthodox, though the intermittent gratuitous dissonance, especially simultaneous natural and sharp on the 6th degree of the scale, betrays an unconcealed impatience with it. The structure of the piece is not especially like Coprario, who tended to a tripartite division: a fugato on a well-characterised 'point' of imitation, chordal or dissonant middle episodes, a final fugato, stronger on insistent rhythm than tune. There does persist a stamp of Coprario on all of Lawes' episodes, such as the petulant interjection at 35, scattered between three of the parts, which is the turning-point of the piece; but the cohesion between them is masterful and new. It was not achieved in one blow. This first version of the piece ran away with its writer in a sprawl of ideas; the later partbook copies (including the composer's own) delete a section that stood before the last, between present bars 48–9, which Lawes rightly felt took too long in steering the piece home.[15] The rejected ideas, however transient, show recurrent patterns, which crop up rehashed in six-part fantasies in *c* and *C*.[16] As it now stands after the deletion, the coda and the diminished intervals of its magnificent 'irrational' bass line (which recalls the extremes through which voices were put in Italian madrigal, from Giaches de Wert onwards) do not suffer the mounted tension to deflate.

The second fantasy then begins in midstream, employing more fluid motion than the first (as often). The overall plan is similar, and would have seemed more so with retention of the excised section; the median interjection of the first piece is extended into a central plateau (23–38) of curved reflective lines, from which the bass is largely

<hr>

[15] Printed in Lawes ed. Lefkowitz (1963) = *MB* XXI, no.2. The composer's own sole surviving partbook for bass line, Add. MS 17798, has at this point the leaf holding the end of this fantasy removed and another, probably in William's hand, inserted in its place. See below in discussion of sett IV for other signs of composer's revisions.

[16] Cf. bars 101–5 (ibid.) with the 1st fantasy a6 in *c*, coda; more extendedly with the 1st fantasy in *C*.

absent, enclosed within peremptory crotchet demands by the upper voices over static bass. The later freedom within the organ accompaniment is only hinted at by the supply of a few basso notes and simplifications of florid string movement; regrettably it does not yet develop explicitly, as one would have liked (and perhaps as the organist extemporised?), but simply doubles the strings at momentous points like the ominous little chromatic ascending figure passed fleetingly upward through the texture (8–10).

Consort Sett III

By the third sett (in c, nos. 74–7), a pattern was emerging of tying the pavan and alman, the more serious cast of dance, closely to the fantasy-movement: the dances being pre-existent, the fantasies took their cue from them. Lawes is the only composer for five to six parts, excepting only the later John Hingeston, composer to the much more mundane Cromwellian court (from about 1651–8), to devise setts made up exactly of the constituents mentioned by Mace. (One thinks too of Matthew Locke's inventiveness in organising suites; except that the fantasy above four parts held no charms for him.[17]) In this case, as can be shown for almost all the dances from the five-part setts, the aires preceded the fantasy movement; certainly with the first aire, which Lawes wrote into the Shirley books in a three-part (Tr–Tr–B) version, and almost as certainly with the other two.[18]

The pavan is found in a partbook set devoted to dances in the new Tr–Tr idiom, either in three-part (Tr–Tr–B–bc) or four-part (Tr–Tr–T–B–bc) form, like the slightly earlier sets belonging to Browne. Since this set, GB-Lbl, Add. MSS 18940–4, is a good source for the music of, and may be close to, Simon Ives, it has been suggested that the pieces could have formed part of the repertory of theatre musicians in the later 1630s, like those at Blackfriars where Ives worked; if so, that would show a surprising readiness in the public audience to come to terms with the Tr–Tr style from the esoteric chamber music.

[17] Hulse (1983); Field (1970).
[18] Lawes ed. Dodd (1966) = SP 38, no. 11; 3-part version of 5-part aire no. 75.

The books contain the well-known piece, 'Whitelocke's coranto', in the settting of which Ives 'helped out' (one guesses considerably) when Bulstrode Whitelocke, a self-important lawyer later in the foreign service for the Commonwealth, felt moved with the inspiration to write one. Whitelocke's own version (perhaps even this was smartened by Ives) has just the Tr–B outline: Ives set it for the Tr–Tr–T–B combination. It could have been something as small as this that led to the commission from Whitelocke for Ives and Lawes to provide the music for the Inns of Courts' masque in 1634, James Shirley's *Triumph of Peace*.[19]

Lawes' pavan is another piece in four-part (Tr–Tr–T–B–bc) form; its key *d*, from which it was transposed down into *c* for the viol consort version, probably presupposes original performance on violins. It stands at the end of a half-century's quotations of Dowland's famous pavan 'Lachrimæ', which, in origin a lute-solo, was then adapted by the composer into what became the most famous song of its era, 'Flow my teares', and finally scored for five strings with lute continuo at the head of a strange and impenetrable pavan-cycle, a septenary dedicated in 1604 to Anne of Denmark, wife of James I. Bandying talk of quotations is not the same as pinning them down; and there is an element of commonplace in Dowland's own original.[20] His genius lay in taking the familiar and laying bare its hidden soul; for, paradoxically, the falling tetrachord he set out in the first phrase of the pavan occurs as a stock figure throughout the literature over this dance's typical slow-moving or static opening bars. Dowland revealed its depths by restating it a third higher in augmentation, and setting beneath it a bass that echoes its rise of a sixth; elements that at least one subtle tribute, by Thomas Tomkins, cleverly copies.[21] Little of that is found in Lawes. The quotation, though, is clear; the organ prominently states the phrase 'Harke you shadowes that in darcknesse dwell' at the beginning of the third strain as if to make the model unmistakable (Ex. 18).

---

[19] Lawes ed. Lefkowitz (1970) contains a generous selection of dances by Ives that fill the gap for music now missing from the masque. See also Holman (1975–6) for a reconstruction of the instrumental portion.

[20] It was recognised for this piece by [Arkwright] (1909–10).

[21] Poulton (1972), see also Pinto (forthcoming *d*).

Ex. 18: Pavan (76)

The rest is removed some way from the linear elegance of Dowland's original. The point of the adaptation lies in the canonic and tortured Tr–Tr duet, which begins gracefully enough with a sinuous version of the theme. By strain two, however (in the relative major, reminiscent of Dowland's 'Neuer may my woes be relieued'), an unrelieved stomp develops over a very sluggish bass line, which throughout has its fair share and more of semibreve and breve note-values and tonic–dominant irresolution. The moment in which it lifts from dominant to leading note (B natural) after a pedal G that had threatened complete immobility beneath increasingly agitated trebles (bar 31) is an overpowering and movingly simple gesture, tendering resignation of effort. The added part throughout is line IV, which apart from an opening imitation worked in has little distinct to offer apart from some passable contrary motion. Within the layers of this inheritance something novel had the chance to hatch. Lawes by borrowing the pavan's potent theme found licence to devise a congenial opening point for his derivative fantasy. It actually is 'Lachrimæ', lapped within juxtaposing overlapping triads (c–e–g and a flat–c–e flat). This feat folds over the two halves of the theme to sound simultaneously (Ex. 19).

Why the adaptation was ingeniously designed to conceal is unclear; perhaps little more than as a tease for fellow-players. What it must intend to show off is the dazzling bow-technique of the

Ex. 19: Fantasy (74)

Part as written

Implied part-writing

Original theme

professional (for all were trained on lyra-viol, to strum the viol chordally with the bow and extract maximum sonority). There is also a sting in the tail of the theme: a flagellum of arpeggiated quavers that follow, and soon discard, the opening germ. Behind the theme's authority Lawes' fantasy comes of age, discarding any instinctive obeisance to inherited techniques. Much of the the counterpoint in this florid style is meretricious work which subverts procedures while appearing to follow them. There is a stiff or pedantic regularity to the disposal of the opening point, one entry neatly assigned to every bar (breve), perhaps necessary for the ear where the matter is so bizarre; but line IV drops out upon the entry of V (bar 5), II on the re-entry of IV (8), so that the texture is light and effectively never more than four-part right up to bar 30, except for a little homophonic interjection at 23 on the dominant. Also on the dominant sticking-point is the first of Lawes' extended and unusually long bass pedals, emphasised by its very early place in the piece (16–20, and implicit in the following three bars too, 21–3, as the bass takes part in an imitation, derived from the sinking sixth-to-dominant, in notes 3–4 of the first point). Building on the prominent moves to the dominant stolen from the pavan, it is still part of the reflection on Dowland.

In contrast to the pavan's immobilised emotion, there is an impetuosity and dash about the whirl of this piece that makes both pavan and fantasy unlike anything previous in the repertoire. Perhaps the trebles jostle each other out of balance and towards confusion, as the quaver flurries permeate the parts towards the end (35 on), but it was early days as yet. The organ part begins to come into its own through a stronger supporting function; ironing out the contours of quaver movement in the strings to support the sound and filling out the sonority in the brief duet and trio passages (bars 23–9) with the odd gesture towards four-part harmony.

The associated aires are not strongly bound in any thematic way to the main couple of this sett (fantasy–pavan), but complement each other handsomely without any marked similarities, except the flat–sharp seventh alternation between the trebles at the approach to the cadences at bars 13 and 11 respectively. Lawes rescued one early piece (no. 75) with which he still felt satisfied, and another (no. 77) that moves more in what one feels as the four-square fashion of the danced alman. Mace, who listed Allmaines and Ayres separately when laying out the forms of 'lessons' , did so with a contradistinction that seems to invert the categories: he considered that Allmaines are simply 'very *Ayrey,* and *Lively*' whereas Ayres differ by being 'commonly *Shorter,* and of a more *Quick, and Nimble* Performance', besides often falling into tripla measures.[22] Distinguishing by absolute speed is a fallible procedure, and one where even pronounced differences should not cause undue concern; but it strikes a little oddly to find him regarding the alman as more 'airy' than the aire itself.

No. 75 has the greater flow of air (or melody), however one classifies it. It also carries a whiff of suspicion that the two trebles may have begun as a single line expanded into a duet, a practice observable elsewhere in Lawes.[23] The two tenor parts also appear to be totally new. Oddly enough this sticks out less and indeed is quite unexpected given the fluency of the passage-work in bars 10–11, where the bass drops out and, in the three-part version of the Shirley Partbooks, leaves the treble duet unsupported.[24]

[22] Mace (1676), 128–9.
[23] See e.g. 'Royall Consort' no. 41, 'Morriss'; and of course the aire from the 5-part viol sett in *a,* no. 73.
[24] Lawes ed. Dodd (1966) = *SP* 38. The Shirley books have no bc surviving, though it of course conceivable that one has long been lost—the set is lacking one partbook at least, to give a full text for the 6-part fantasy section and complete some 2-part fantasies by Coprario.

The accompanying aire (no. 77) has its own problematic past—
or was it a future? It occurs in some mid-century partbooks containing a mixed bag of remarkable Italian-English vocal repertoire, both
sacred and secular items, that begin with a group of English anthems
attributable to Henry Lawes: only the first, which sets Thomas Carew's
paraphrase of Psalm 137, 'Sitting by the streames that glyde', bears
an ascription to Henry; but they are stylistically and obviously a group,
as the further link with William proves. Date of copying (let alone
composition of the pieces) is unclear on surviving evidence, but appears to be Commonwealth, c.1655, ten years after William's death.
The anthem that carries aire no. 77 as a 'simphony', 'My soule the
Great God['s] praises singes', is another paraphrase by Carew, of
Psalm 104: the two strains of the dance were sundered and severally
commandeered as simphonies (or ritornelli) between the verses performed by the five voices. This version is a Tr–B skeleton, though
after common practice it could have been used as the basis for a
five-part ensemble in the usual violin's Tr–A–T–Bar–B scoring. What
one would dearly like to know is date of composition. Carew apparently wrote his psalm-paraphrases in the 1620s in a fright, convalesc-
ing from venereal disease. One of them was set by Henry before the
wars (now not extant, but listed in Chapel Royal use by 1635: 'Make
the great God thy fort', Psalm 46); the question is, what date applies
to the others we do have? The two from the MS set, now GB-Lbl,
Add. MS 31434, appeared in a libretto dated 1655 for a (Cecilian?)
festival on 22 November in that year.[25] One, if only one, reason to
think it much earlier, is the state of William's alman. It could of course
be Henry's in origin; the two brothers lived (from time to time, at
least) in each other's pockets, and operated the Hobson-Jobson principle with regards to some musical enterprises. Whoever devised it,
though, it appears from the unrevised form of the second strain—as
so often, lengthened, and elaborated round the final cadence by
William when he reset it for the (Tr–Tr) five-viol consort—that the

[25] Henry's settings discussed in Pinto (1981). The libretto, formerly in the possession of the Egerton family, with whom Henry and John Milton are for ever closely
associated through *Comus*, was acquired by San Marino's Huntington Library. The
opening vocal phrase of Henry's setting of Psalm 104 is underlaid by a basso line
that makes reference to the alman bass; a sign that the dance came first?

Ex. 20: My soule the Great God

attr. Henry Lawes

86

verse-anthem version is the earlier (Ex. 20: the five-part version gives the main treble line as line II). As noted above, Lawes may in reworking this second strain have cannibalised a little alman found (also much later) in Playford's dance-publication, *Court-Ayres* (1655) no. 137 (Dodd no. 233) (Ex. 21; see also Chapter II, Ex. 14a). It is useful to see how, sometimes at least, ideas stayed with him for recogitation if he felt them undernourished, and could burgeon in this way. There is in the final version some common ground with the Royall Consort's type of alman, but also a certain difference in disposal of weight, a thoughtfulness in the elongation of the phrasing, from bars 17 on, and especially from 23, that betrays how wide the narrow gap has become.

Ex. 21: Alman (233)

Consort Sett IV

In many ways (emotionally as well) the least complicated of all, the sett in *F* seizes on the discovery of how best to 'lyrify' a theme, as carried out in the fantasy of the previous sett, and blithely puts it through its paces. There is no disguised core to the main theme yet uncovered. It resembles if anything the well-known 'flaxen-headed ploughboy', quite fortuitously; but what possibly sparked it is a reinterpretation of the theme and method of a six-part fantasy by Charles

Coleman (no. 3, also in F)[26] That was a model which cannot claim to be new repertoire of the 1630s; sources in which Coleman's five extant six-part works appear cannot be much after the later '20s, even if Lawes may well have turned to them for a hint or two when mulling over his own six-part plans. If there is a parallel here it must be that Lawes saw an opportunity to condense Coleman's initial point into a tighter sequence of seven crotchets that cog-wheel down in overlapping thirds, before spinning off into quavers as in the previous fantasy in c. The walk on which Coleman took it involved augmentation into double values and a meander into flat keys, as far as f (minor), before abruptly shifting pace and abandoning the principal theme of what had threatened to become a harangue, a little beyond the halfway point, at bar 42 (Ex. 22a–b).

Lawes had very little use for anything so academic as augmentation, but had a keen sense of key-relations, tempered by the limitations of the prospective listener.[27] He does take up the idea of modulation, and pushes his own version of the point into as ranging a voyage as he felt useful: relative minor at bar 12, before the initial point peters out into accompanied treble antiphony; and between 27 and 37 into the flat side of the key-cycle, c, f and A flat before securing a rapid passage out by brandishing a quiverful of quavers (34–5). Counterpoint is not really the operative word where the lower parts (especially the tenors) are become so rhythmically subservient to the exigencies of the treble lines. There is, though (as if to confute expectations), one teasing interplay, between the trebles naturally, when line I in bars 41–2 repeats bars 37–9 from line II in diminution.

The pavan of the sett (79) is, like the alman (80), a reworked four-parter from the early sett in G that preceded the Royall Consort. This time a very little of the material from the original tenor (line III out of the four bowed parts) is assigned to the new IV (out of five lines); less out of a sense of fair play in sharing the polyphonic interest than out of a desire to lighten the dense texture by inserting line

[26] Coleman ed. Davis (1971) = *SP* 81.
[27] Dent (1928) first pointed out the novel coherence to the key-schemes found in William's public masque music.

Ex. 22a: Fantasy no. 3 a6   Charles Coleman

Ex. 22b: Fantasy (78)

III in a higher niche. The trouble arose from lowering by a further tone the pitch of an already low-lying piece, presumably to give a whole consort of viols some open strings to bound off. This, though, applies only to the alman, as at bars 35–6 in the trebles. Lawes seemingly considered the two dances an unsunderable couple and felt willing to allow the sombre result—at first. There are some striking differences between the autograph scorebook and the various playing parts that survive, in these two pieces most out of all from the five-part setts, which suggest he may have had second (or even third)

thoughts. Numerous octave transpositions in the tenor lines, mainly III, for these dances, seem to show that revision of the texture continued without being noted down in score. Changes may have been made *ad lib* on more than one occasion, to account for variation between partbook copies. To what extent they may be considered authenticable is an open question; but revisions or seeming revisions are increasingly a feature of the partbook copies from this point on.[28]

In the pavan, Lawes must have congratulated himself on expressing the essence of the genre, as part of a tradition that by this point had a history of close on a century. A hunt for exact models is probably an irrelevance where the inheritance is so profuse. The leisurely opening span of melody is given to line II, prefigured by I. It is the sort of rising fifth-to-sixth typical of pavans, which need to set their immediate direction without disturbing the repose of their harmonic base. Lawes, naturally, takes ideas of movement and repose so far as they will readily be combined; in this case 4 bars over a pedal F (present or implicit), followed by one of those little chromatic bass phrases sinking through the semitones just in order to point the harmonic direction (the arrival at the dominant). It is a very satisfying pastoral opening, mainly through the combination of steady sonority with purposeful movement between the treble lines. The opening treble line stresses, as often, the fifth and sixth of the scale, where it peaks in its rise and fall. The added part, line IV, affirms this movement in the simplest possible way by its added sixth on the last minim beat of bar 1, which emphasises the autumnal ripeness heavy in the air. Giving line III its quota of harmony to fill does result in some successes: the bold augmented fourth at bars 22–3 to give the simulacrum of parallel fifths, seen all too blatantly in the organ part, was worth the effort (if it had been the composer's original intention, it was not visible in the four-part version).

---

[28] Textual commentary in Lawes ed. Pinto (1979) includes all major discrepancies between autograph score and non-autograph copies. Only one partbook survives from a set in the composer's own hand, GB-Lbl, Add. MS 17798, which attests that the 'revisions' found in other partbooks are to some extent the composer's own.

Strain two brings in the doubts inherent in the contrasting relative minor, rather as the mid-section of the fantasy; strain three forces an altogether abrupt solution to the business of returning to key. A disjointed key-shift of a tone is made at the strain's beginning (bar 28), from *d* (with Picardy third) to *C*, which emphasises a shift in mood as well. The piece does not fall into the pavan-alman class, but instead, this third strain more or less pushes into the listener's hands an embedded alman to make do for a conclusion, in jaunty but gently dotted quavers that emerge gradually after bar 30 (by 33–4 at latest: the given mixture of dotted and undotted suggests an *inégalité*, as so often) and persist until the end. How successful prove the juxtapositions made by this strain, and the indecisions about sonorities shown in the tampering with pitch in the middle parts, depends on one's passion for good joinery; but it is a serviceable piece of *bricolage* (to say no more), and obviously continued by and large to satisfy its composer.

To a lesser degree the same problem over the tessitura of the tenor (line III) crops up in the alman of the sett (no. 80), another revamped piece from the early sett in *G* (Ex. 23a); but here it seems easier to ignore, in an aire of rare distinction. Almost certainly it owes its theme to an earlier alman by the court veteran Robert Johnson II, well known in various scorings, especially lute and keyboard (Ex. 23b). Johnson's original has been claimed as a masque dance, from

Ex. 23a: Alman (80)

Ex. 23b: Mʳ Johnsonns Almayne   Robert Johnson II

Ben Jonson's 'Oberon', performed in honour of Henry Prince of Wales on 1 January 1611, though hard proof for this is lacking.[29] It is, though, a theme clearly in the court tradition, crystallinely spun out between the very smooth trebles of strain one as they constantly cede to each other, over a bass even more linear. (Bars 7–16, once octave transitions are ironed out, form one single falling phrase that includes only four simple upward motions of a tone or less).

In rescoring this piece from four to five parts Lawes had no work except for the extra line IV, though he slowed the pace mildly by adding a semibreve bars-worth at the end of the first strain, that overlays a nagging rhythmic similarity, in line II, to the final cadence of

[29] Pinto (1981), 22, on a claim made in Cutts (1960). See also Johnson (1972) and Chan (1980). Holman (1978) refers to the keyboard setting of GB-Och 1113, which was known earlier to Arkwright; it is reproduced in Pinto (1981). Ex. 23a is taken from GB-Lbl, Add. MS 36661, f. 54v, 'Mʳ Johnsonns Almayne'. A further source for Johnson's piece has since been uncovered in an English lute MS c.1615, formerly Berlin, Preussische Staatsbibliothek, Musikabteilung, Mus. MS 40641, and at present Kraków, Biblioteka Jagiellónska (unnumbered), f. 9v, 'Ballett'.

the second strain in line I. The showy, very ornamental semiquaver figures of the second strain are of course like nothing in Johnson, and little more than written-out graces; except that they build up a head of steam toward the significant point of bar 33, where the trebles in canonic thirds are underpinned by a chromatically sinking bass which picks up in diminution the same figure from bar 5 of the pavan. The trebles therefore may also contain a reminiscence of their former interlocking amble over this figure at the pavan's opening; though without the clue in the bass part it would not have been spottable, owing to transposition into the higher octave and addition of semiquaver figures.

Consort Sett V

The sett in C is the furthest Lawes took the tendency to figuration for its own sake that probably outraged—still outrages—some listeners as much as it has diverted others. The fantasy (no. 81) is the shortest of them all at a mere 39 breves. From the Sett in *a* onwards, these movements which traditionalists might have expected to form the *entrée* of the setts had been contracting steadily and alarmingly, and bring to mind Nietzsche's prescription for the best way to take a dose of philosophy: quick in, quick out, like a cold bath. In it, was Lawes clowning to the more boisterous of his acquaintances? He went to some trouble to deliver the initial shock, the headlong lemming rush of the fantasy's first point. The sheer pace of it weakens recognition of how it is the starkest (but far from the darkest) of his themes. Octave, fifth and seventh are stressed in that order, on which pinnacle it threatens to impale itself until it weakens and curls back to the sixth in bar 7 (line II), over an excruciating diminished octave caused by a bass G sharp. This sourness contracts into an especially rancid dominant seventh in bar 8, as the bass turns the tight corner into relative minor (and prepares the ground for a treble octave leap of b'–b", unusual in the key-context and in stretching treble fingering patterns). If the bass then fades out, allowing a peaceful return to key, it is only to thump out the more noticeably a firmer departure for the octave figure on its re-entry in bar 10. Initially in fact a two-octave leap, it dissolves the theme and some developing linear fourths (visible best in the organ accompaniment) in a bounding and plunging, which actually pose little technical problem to a lyra-violist, but disrupt the semblance of a contrapuntal fabric beyond repair. From bar 19 pretty well to the end, various homophonic mixtures are taken in remedy, with a slim chance of recuperation for the patient.

Lawes worked himself into this extremity deliberately. He went through his score for what is now the first section, to mid-bar 10, slashing all note-values by half (though no other alteration was made). The same change is found in his extant bass partbook, though not, interestingly, the organ book, where only the speedier version is found. It implies an early change, but one made only after the piece had been tested on colleagues in rehearsal. It means that the crux at bars 7–8 is intended to arrive and depart before the listener has had time to adjust, leaving the ear stranded. Possibly the undoubted force of the piece's first half (persisting beyond the turn into tonic minor at bar 20) is dissipated by the inconclusiveness of what follows. The treble antiphony acts effectively up to a baying canon in the minor, 20–6, but then the second treble and bass drop out during the introduction of weak dotted undulations in the remaining lines. The pace is not recaptured before the final unwinding from 34 on, introduced by one of Lawes' idiosyncrasies: a solitary bass semibreve inserted on an unexpected scale-degree to steer the parts back through a plagal cadence. Repeated high calls on e″ sound the last post in the trebles over the simplest of chordal progressions, ending with 6–3, 5–3.

Many of the fantasy's puzzling features may proceed from a dependence on, and decision to correlate with, the accompanying pavan; but that piece too has its enigmas. Models do exist in a general way for the pavan–alman pairing in C, principally that by Richard Dering, which in its Tr–Tr scoring is an evolutionary stage in the abstract chamber pavan's transformation between Alfonso Ferrabosco II and Lawes. Dering with Mico (his successor in the employ of Queen Henrietta Maria) show the state of the art c.1625 and to an extent prefigure the static bass-lines, accumulation of frothy detail in the trebles, transitions to unusual key-destinations which Lawes shows too (see Ex. 24a–b for incipits).[30] The comparison, though, only makes Lawes look more alien.

Ex. 24a: Pavan no. 4   Richard Dering

Ex. 24b: Pavan (82)

This piece is the only one of his five-part dances that is *un*known in a smaller-scale version, albeit the Tr–Tr–B structure is as clearly visible as ever. If the minimal opening point (sol–fa–sol against ut–re–ut) has a parallel, it is a fleeting opening one with the first of his own dances ever copied by Lawes: in G, as quoted in Chapter I. The trebles respond antiphonally, follow one another in brief canon, saunter in supportive thirds as sedately as one could wish. They also indulge in some disjunct steps, in the course of this gimell that yields precedence between the members of the pair, and produces the appearance of a single (if segmented) melody: a constant trait of the Royall Consort too, fastened on (perhaps not with complete approval)

---

[30] Mico ed. Hanley (1994); Dering, P–A pair in Nicholson (1981).

by Ernst Meyer. The effect is of a cloying, lingering taste of E, the third degree of the key, and in strains two to three of excessive dotted undulatory motion—the effect of the fantasy bars 26–33 repeated (or else heralded, if the pavan came first). Diminished octaves and soured sharps have a central place in the third strain, bars 25–6, equivalent to those in the fantasy bars 7–8; but here lingered on and even redoubled (on bass pitches c sharp and G sharp), as though the accumulated gall cannot be totally overlaid with the honey, even by a repeat of the trivial quaver roulades from strain two. Finally, from mid-bar 29 till the end, there comes a brief homophonic episode accompanied by very full organ chords that through the mediant move abruptly into, and as abruptly out of, a chord of B. An *envoi* to the writing of five-part setts, penned in gathering impatience, perhaps? Its homophony relates to the *faux-naif* final cadence of the fantasy, but it is still an unprecedented method of despatching a pavan (except that, by coincidence or no, a similar chordal *envoi* presents itself at the end of Jenkins' six-part 'Bell Pavan', after the elegiac galliard-like bell-passage). Gordon Dodd suggested, eminently sensibly under the circumstances, that players should omit this valediction from the first time through the strain and just play it once finally, following the second-time repeat. All very well, though after this 'loth to depart' one makes a second round of lingering farewells, in the aire (83).

This, another of the early works from the Shirley books, brings full circle Lawes' picaresque encounter with the five-part ensemble.[31] From the imitatively spaced entries of its opening bars, it immediately makes itself felt as less a dance, in its first strain at least, than the 'airier', more melodious type of alman. Both the tenor parts are extraneous to the original Tr–Tr–B scoring; they add little of vital interest, excepting an extraordinary note-cluster in bar 9 where the four adjacent tones e–a (including the held chord in the organ part) fleetingly collide over bass C. They create, though, a new bar 1, an inserted false entry; it anticipates the bass real statement on pitch c, and wrong-foots the treble's prerogative: in consequence the clear harmonic logic of the treble–bass interplay is obscured by the faltering

---

[31] 3-part version in Lawes ed. Dodd (1966) = *SP* 38, no. 13 (see n. 18).

of the rhythmic step. If the balance is thrown awry, in a piece of this unfailing good humour the momentary lurch can hardly be held against the host of the party as a lapse gross enough to undermine the festive spirit. The opening point of imitation may be linked to figuration at the pavan's beginning (cf. line V, pavan bars 3–4 with aire 5–7); if so it poses the question whether the pavan was the afterthought, and whether, in this sett as in the previous one in F, the inspiration flowed backwards (as it were), towards the initial fantasy, from the slightest member of the group, the final alman. (Certainly the pavan could function without real loss in a Tr–Tr–B form, just as the aire had previously).

Strain two of the alman is a total replacement. The Shirley version had meandered most unhappily into the relative minor, and out again by dint of a third strain, tripla-fashion (which is the sort of form peculiar to orchestrated masque-dances, though no specific occasions are known for such employ of those early three-part versions).[32] Strain two of the five-part version is a triumph: beginning with an incisive repeated-crotchet formula typical of the coming six-part almans, Lawes consummates the two-treble partnership by an extended play on the implications of the mediant E. As had never quite developed in the fantasy and pavan, the phrasing has been allowed its own time to mature and breathe with full lungs. The repeated treble calls (heard too in the finale of the fantasy) have an echo from afar of the *stile concitato*, the harshly rhythmic genus of composition devised by Monteverdi to represent the emotions of battle. Direct influence at this time is improbable, although Walter Porter in the Chapel Royal, whom Henry if not William will have known, was by his own statement a pupil of Monteverdi.

The five-part setts end here with possibly the most extended pedal that Lawes ever penned, out of many: eleven semibreves on the dominant in the bass, foreshadowed by a further two in the treble *in alt* to make thirteen, bids fair to make the record books (the only contender is at the beginning of the six-part sequence in the alman in g, no. 86; for which see below). One can compare other pedals, such as alman no. 51 in the Royall Consort, where similar games of harsh

---

[32] Ibid. See Sabol (1978) on the structure of masque dances.

canon over a static bass are played out (the pedal there is a mere five semibreves). In bar 27 of the Royall Consort piece there is a jokey intrusion of f' sharp (pointed out by Layton Ring), intended to lead the ear astray with a misleading turn to dominant harmonies,which are wilfully introduced, principally for the piquancy of extra dissonance. This sharp seventh in the dominant occurs also in the viol aire, bar 41—in the organ only, and wisely positioned less close to the end, at a point where downward treble figures are replaced by a final upward surge. It is found moreover in the violin setts: the 'close' (coda) to the 4th sett for one violin ends with just this little quirk of an f"sharp as grace-note to a chord of C. [33]

One presumes that this revised second strain to the alman, from its status as amplification of the same idea, actually postdated the Royall Consort sett in C—which, as suggested above, was probably composed simultaneously in both 'old' and 'new' versions. It begins to suggest a timetable for coordinating evidence for composition of the various chief works. One reason for the brevity of sett V in C may simply be that Lawes was growing bored with five-part music and looking for a further challenge in the six-part field. There are features in common with the six-part works that begin to reveal themselves out of this shell, as if through a hatching process. Early work in adapted form it may be, but the insistent rhythmic pattern of the aire's first strain, a repetitive group of two quavers and crotchet that sound like a personal motto, come to prominence in the six-part setts. The closeness of approach employed in the final cadence of the five-part fantasy to those of the six-part fantasies in the same key suggests that if their composition was not synchronous, it was allied in purpose. Into the same time-band may come the fantasies for the Royall Consort at its fullest, six-part, stretch. Lawes had presumably tired of devising setts around pre-existent dances, and saw a chance to use Tr–Tr–B–B techniques to make the fantasy once again the most significant member of a sett: he was casting an inventive mind ahead and planning how to expand the same techniques for the six-part ensemble.

---

[33] Lawes ed. Pinto (1991), no. 4(c), bar 55. See also Ring (1972).

IV
The Six-part Setts

The main insight into Lawes' working methods for both five-part and six-part setts relies on examining his two scorebooks, now housed in the Music Sc hool collection of the Bodleian Library, Oxford, Music School MSS B.2 and B.3; probably a bequest owed to the generosity of his brother Henry who may have wished thus to perpetuate his memory. (He will have given the organbook and partbooks for violin works as well, but immethodically enough, and frustratingly for us, not the parts for the viol setts; these he kept, perhaps prizing them above the rest.) Musicians after the 1630s seem to have become worried about posterity as never before, in the material way of prudently securing their *Nachlass*. Perhaps instrumental music was recognised to give fleeting fame in a way not urgently apparent to previous composers, who may have worked chiefly in the service of the liturgy, or (if player-composers of instrumental works) in the employ of patrons who might be relied on to maintain the honour of their house and include their domestics in its aura. The mid-century upheavals were obviously a big part in the change in attitude, after the cream of the profession had found incidental employment dry up (just when the court ceased to be the cynosure for musical fashions), and thereon were forced to turn to music lessons as a shift. (Hence too the impressive publishing record of John Playford during the Commonwealth years, that gave a remarkably censor-free stimulus to printing and publishing of most sorts—even the arcane astrological texts that ecclesiastical censorship before the wars had suppressed.)

Another thing is owed to Henry: the original loan of his scorebook to his younger brother. MS B.2 bears the initials W.L., but B.3 is stamped H.L.; nonetheless William took it for a supplementary score-volume.[1] It

[1] Similar books are known. That of Locke's autograph viol music is one, an identification owed to Robert Ford: GB-Lbl, Add.MS 17801, which has the same stamp of royal arms as MSS B.2–B.3, but lacks initials. The same stamp occurs on GB-Lbl, MS RM 24.k.3 and elsewhere : see Lawes ed. Pinto (1991) = *MB* LX, 114. What was probably a scorebook of this sort belonged to John Tomkins, and subsequently to Thomas his half-brother: see Willetts (1991), 35.

contains principally the Royall Consort, setts 1–6 as rescored in the new version, preceded by a section wherein it was intended to lay out most if not all of the six-part viol consorts; the two activities may have been simultaneous. Spacing problems afflicted William thereafter. He may not at first have intended the Royall Consort to run over target by the addition of fantasy or pavan movements, and need extra space in the H.L. volume at the beginning of the sequence (for the fantasy in *d*, for example): sorting out the order and contents for the *d–D* setts was perhaps not planned in advance, and caused more trouble than bargained for.) Since every spare scrap was being taken up for the revised 'Royall' pieces, William turned back to the other (W.L.) scorebook to finish off the six-part viol setts. In this more miscellaneous company space was left, even if some sandwiching was necessary.

An order of scoring into these books for the six-part setts is then clear: first the setts in *C*, *G*, *F* found in Henry's book. The *g* sett may actually have preceded the *C* sett, apparently there beforehand, since it could have been copied in later onto the extremity of a first few untouched leaves; at any rate, William put the *g* sett first when inserting the first three six-part setts to follow the five-part in his organbook, and obviously intended it to have pride of place. (The 1630s saw the emergence of sett-design founded on a scalar order, starting often from *g–G*, for Gamut, and passing up the notes of the keyboard in varying ways. Jenkins used various systems including the array *g–d–a–e–c–F–B* flat, but also others beginning on *F*. Lawes began from *g* in his violin setts, and may have intended parallel sequences beginning from *g* in the viol setts too; but if so, the logic of the heart ran away with this plan, which diverged to include the six-part *B* flat pieces.) He lastly added untidily around the edges outwards of the organbook the setts in *B* flat and *c*, which undoubtedly reflects the order of composition.

Consort Sett VI

A pavan to head the six-part sequence must have been designed to impress and be imposing, and such is the pavan in *g* (no. 84). To find a real six-part pavan is a rarity, even hidden amidst the itself

100

endangered species of fantasies on that scale.[2] In England, unlike Germany where William Brade made a substantial contribution, obviously appreciated there, to the six-part store, there can have been little demand for danceable pavans in the scoring, and one has to imagine some uncustomary function for the three pavan–galliard pairs that survive by Byrd, Gibbons and Tomkins. It is all too clear that Lawes could not have intended his unwieldy and baroque piece to set any dancer's foot a-tapping; there is practically nothing in it reminiscent of dance, beyond the regulation three-strain form. None of his six-part dances (all almans otherwise) have any known alternative scoring, as is the case with the five-part pieces, excepting only the final pavan; we have therefore moved completely into the realm of the purely aural.[3]

There is between the constituent pieces of the sett in g a new organic cohesion, a more ingrained allusiveness between the pieces: it begins immediately as the pavan rises to a peak in bars 6–7, which foreshadow the culmination of the fantasy's first section (bars 10–11). Thematically the pavan-opening is distinct from that of the fantasy, but it plays with a familiar preoccupation of Lawes underlying the fantasy too: the overlapping triads, pointing up to the seventh of the scale or down to the submediant. The business of the pavan's first 5 bars is a simple two-voiced affair between I and VI to which all else is subordinated (Ex. 25). The untimely entry of line V, anticipating this probing dialogue, is just an unwanted by-product of the grouping of the lines into three natural pairs. Where a simple basso

Ex. 25: Pavan (84)

[2] Single pavans a6 occur by Cranford (2 examples), Jacob Ørn (a migrant visitor to English shores), Jenkins of course; Leetherland, Peter Phillips and William White.
[3] Dodd (1991) is recommended for an inimitable study of the sett, the terms of which are not emulated here.

line is wanted, it leaves one of the bass pair shifting foot or biding time, in the saturated six-part texture. Line V cannot be intended to obtrude (oddly enough the same detail recurs in the first bar of Jenkins' six-part 'Bell Pavan'). This inconclusive dialogue is initiated by a falling third, initially a simple triad which the bass imitation pushes down to the submediant. It seems a very little gesture to pick a quarrel over, especially since it simply wanders back to the key-note via a small chromatic inflection; yet out of it arises an immensely petulant storm of quavers, one that is repeated in the fantasy. The journey to dominant or submediant and back, that strikes one as so inconsequential for a cause of all this 'wuthering', held some special significance for Lawes: something very similar occurs in the open-ing bars of his latin psalm-setting for three voices as printed by his brother in the posthumous *Choice Psalmes*, no. 27: 'Ne irascaris

Ex. 26: Ne irascaris Domine

Domine' (Isaiah 64. 9–10)—not the only harmonic likeness between the pieces (Ex. 26).

Six-part writing, testing for most composers, put Lawes on his mettle. There is a new ampleness to the phrasing, strikingly distinct from the pell-mell staccato of the five-part fantasies. The doubled basses offered an opportunity taken firmly for pairing them with antiphonal trebles, even more than in the Royall Consort, where one of the bass pair was always on call for tenor-range duties. The organ part too comes into its own with an extended role in accompanying duets (as at bars 9–10) and interpreting the texture (as at 16–17 where it has an imitative entry of its own), rather than shadowing it in short-score fashion, the duty in which all other writers in six parts had been content to leave it—or so it appears from surviving sources, since we are not overblest with composers' own playing parts. One distinctive feature of this sett is the pairing into three very separate levels, that prefer to respond internally rather than imitate across the ranks. The result is a very lucid texture, far from dense even when thickest or most rapid, and versatile at devising special effects rarely if ever heard in a pavan before: the duets, the free-range basses that hop around lyra-fashion (strain two), the dramatic near-silences at interrupted cadences where a bass alone is left bearing the strain.

Another detail that recalls the psalms is the falling chromatic bass-line. First heard briefly at 9–10, it creeps in at the end of strain two (during a very stratified moment, where tenors roll quavers between them, and trebles descend on oddly hocketing minims). Its re-emergence in the third strain, heralded by a contorted moment in bar 32 (where the bass f sharp could be interpreted as a g flat), gives rise to Lawes' longest falling chromatic line, in V, bars 35–8, almost up to the weeping coda. Longest, that is, except for being equalled by a passage from another psalm on the sore-weeping theme, 'Judah in exile wanders', part two of 'How like a widow', to a text from Lamentations (Ex. 27).[4] A further example of self-quotation comes in the Royall Consort pavan in *a* (no. 42, bars 16–17), a 'Gershwin' effect that was placed here at the end of the first strain, but in the pavan in *g* was wisely reserved for the end, bars 43–4 (Ex. 28a–b). Another

---

[4] Quoted in Lefkowitz (1960), 240–1. The lament bass is usually in *g*: Rostand (1979).

Ex. 27: Judah in exile wanders

notable similarity is with a phrase from the Royall Consort pavan in C, beginning of the third strain, which has a kindred movement to the start of this pavan's third strain: an early cadence into the dominant and immediate recourse to crotchet dance rhythms as a means of liberation (Ex. 28c–d). The similarities makes it probable that the three pieces were written close in time, the viol-consort version being the more considered and latest working of these phrases.

Some striking links between Jenkins and Lawes in the following fantasy emerge, when one takes note of the six-part, 'Series II' pieces by Jenkins.[5] Despite uncertainty over dating, there is a strong

[5] Ashbee (1992), 166–85.

Ex. 28a: Pavan (84)

Ex. 28b: Pavan (42)

chance on available (mainly internal) evidence that these works by Jenkins, comprising the two In Nomines, the two pavans and nos. 9–10 out of the fantasies, are lateish; from which one could infer a dating

Ex. 28c: Pavan (49)

Ex. 28d: Pavan (84)

around 1640 and the time of the parallel pieces by Lawes. The two men had known each other since 1634 at latest, when they both participated as favoured performers in the *Triumph of Peace*. A coincidence that cannot be total chance is their turning back to both the six-part pavan, and also the In Nomine, two otherwise outmoded forms.[6] It is obvious too that the In Nomines by Jenkins are linked through their key, and perhaps head-motif as well to the accompanying two fantasies, in *e* and *g*. It increases the chance that they result from direct association with Lawes, and (whatever the cross-influences) that the older man was attempting to outdo the younger at his own game, the use of disjunct angular themes and a spicier harmonic palette. This Jenkins achieves inimitably, at the expense of only a few atypical roughnesses. Wisely he avoided extremes, smoothing out the linear angularities and restricting increase of dissonance to passing-notes, in his wonderful, 'ever-flowing' vein so unlike the pebbly crotchety note-against-note counterpoint that was the younger man's second-rate (in contrapuntal terms) inheritance from Coprario. The theme of the *g* fantasies by the two men belongs to an extended family (Gordon Dodd compares Ferrabosco II, four-part fantasy no. 5), but Lawes stamps it personally by stretching it over his usual Procrustean frame: towards the submediant in the first bass entry, as in the pavan, and upwards to the seventh in the first treble.

Other ingredients in the Lawes dish, some typical, a few novel, soon appear. A dramatic pedal over bass D promotes hacking false relations above, on the minor–major third. This is interrupted by a deceptive cadence onto E flat and the emergence of very independent organ texture, backing a sequence (bars 21–37) of concertante bass duets interlarded with a high quartet. This section, like the whole sett, is notable for the extent to which the three levels of parts are segregated, and the lack of prominence enjoyed by the tenor pair (a mere semibreve's-worth at bar 31). The extent to which the pairs of parts hunt in thirds is also unusual, and possibly refers back to the move towards the submediant of E flat that characterised both the pavan and fantasy openings. It is the basses who have the lion's share, beginning with their foot-stamping in 21, and these grumblings are

---

[6] North thought that Jenkins was the last composer to attempt an In Nomine, as may well have been the case (assuming that Lawes was his inspirer in this genre), excepting only for the very late two 6- and 7-part pieces by Henry Purcell that were seemingly unknown in their own time to connoisseurs: North ed. Wilson (1959), 287; Ashbee (1992), 166–85.

absent for less than seven bars out of the sixteen. The material spreads out into a repeated-note theme that untwines into falling fourths, echoing more diffusely the unwinding strands in the last section of the pavan, and omitting the chromatics. As before, it leads to further interrupted cadences, agitated and contorted interjections, and then a return of sighing downward thirds in the upper voices over slow-moving and agonised bass progressions, applauded by Lefkowitz as quintessential Lawes.[7] But just at the point (bar 49) where the piece seems to have run out of steam by a weak retreat back to key involving an unorthodox shift out of relative major, Lawes launches out into a combination of many of the preceding troubling woes; the falling third gives way immediately to strings of paired crotchets that with mallet-like persistence knock at the material of the initial theme. The bass slides down the chromatic tetrachord to pedal Ds, and juxtaposed (though not simultaneous) minor–major false relations bring back memories of the earlier pedal. The final cadence continues the unceasing drama by winding into the final note with one of Lawes' most arresting cadences, where through a linear subterfuge he avoids a straight plagal cadence on c–g by pushing down to A flat.

The breathtaking rapidity of the five-part fantasy sketches has expanded into a richer, fuller canvas, on which the detail is less tightly controlled by a need to maintain the pretence of counterpoint. This has its forebears of course: the exceptional terracing into 3 pairs of equal voices is a feature also to an exceptional degree in six-part fantasy no. 2 by the late Jacobean William White; but Lawes' use of this type of division to create a cumulative argument surpasses static antithetical displays of sequential figuration.[8] It makes the whole piece into an enormously potent statement—but of what? Gordon Dodd found in it 'a mysterious struggle for power', set in a mood of 'obsessive agitation and anguish'.[9] It is clear that the indecisive repeated notes of the fantasy's opening, and the wavering found at the pavan's beginning between stark *g* tonality and the warmer *E* flat (which

---

[7] Lefkowiz (1960), 58–62.
[8] White's piece in Coates and Dart (1955) = *MB* IX, no.83; also in the complete 6-part fantasies. Dodd finds further thematic similarities between Lawes' 5-part fantasy in *a* (no. 71) and White's 5-part fantasy no. 1, 'Diapente'.
[9] Dodd (1991), 52–61.

later, in the sett in *c*, also stands for reassurance), are symptomatic of very polarised elemental forces, felt with Lear-like intensity. It reminds one listener most of the straining after unheard music evident in *Wuthering Heights*, as captured felicitously in *The Common Reader* by Virginia Woolf: a 'gigantic ambition, a struggle, half thwarted but of superb conviction, to say something', through the interplay of parts, 'which is not merely "I love" or "I hate", but "we, the whole human race" and "you, the eternal powers..."'; the sentence remains unfinished'.[10] One is emboldened to think of Lawes in similar comprehensive terms simply by the way in which his feeling for key enfolds the motivic language which he breathed, and projects it in such cogent flights of fluent melody. All the elements of composition available to him, in other words, seem to be so effectively cohesive.

In the alman too, the stratification of lines and of their material is clear in the opening five bars. Apart from this striking motif, the brief opening section flings around a not-so-striking set of motifs derived from the preceding pieces (bars 8–13, the move to the dominant as the trebles reach the heights, was heard in the pavan, 4–7, and fantasy, 9–11). It is the extended second strain, three times the length of the first, that is unforgettable once heard. It begins sanely enough (bar 18), with a rhythmic and melodic formulation reminiscent of the five-part alman in C (another sign that the six-part sequence followed on closely in time from the five-part?). By 23 this has dissolved into an unusual treble dialogue accompanied by a basso line, with a higher bass shadowing the trebles rather as in the Royall Consort (and tenors provide dissonant filler, as so often). At bar 28, however, right up to 43 and the penultimate note, the basses rear up and overpower the texture with a series of alternating two-octave vaults off their low D. The rate at which these are made whips up corresponding frenzy in the upper voices: once a bar (28) turns quickly (at 30) into twice a bar, after which it diminishes until 37–41. The tenors for once break out, into independent quaver runlets (29), communicated to the trebles in 37. Descending chromatics, simultaneous false relations, make their final banshee return before diminishing to

10 As reprinted in Jean-Pierre Petit (ed.) *Emily Brontë A Critical Anthology* (Harmondsworth, 1973), 74.

a conquered whimper. It is a unique effect and without any real parallel, and created by the simplest of tricks, use of the resonant open D string. Presumably this was the piece, together with the fantasy, that impressed Percy Grainger hugely when Dolmetsch introduced him to a sett; on the evening of 22 July 1931 and again a week later, whereafter Grainger wrote his thanks in glowing terms for acquainting him with the fantasy; 'certainly one of the most glorious and subtle compositions of any school or any period'. It was those two pieces that Grainger later scored for orchestra, for publication in the United States, omitting the pavan.[11] Grainger incidentally showed sympathy for the sonorities by placing beneath the cellos a ripieno double bass to make good the lack of a low D open-string effect.

Consort Sett VII

The sett in C begins with another example of liberation from convention.[12] Block-harmony openings in fantasy are known, though uncommon; there is a striking example by Lupo, also in 6 parts (his no. 5).[13] Lawes' opening, though, is closer to a habit of the chamber pavan, the pre-entry of a treble voice with an imitative point or dominant line (Ex. 29).[14] Rather even than pavan, one might rewrite this prelude of 18 bars as if it opened the fantasy of a violin sett; transposed a tone higher into D , and with perhaps the organ part filled out a little.[15] In a gesture of simplicity and economy which contains the seeds of much to come, line I outlines the leisurely rising four-note phrase, e'–a', a semibreve ahead of the imitation in line II. In conjunction with the basso line rising the fifth c–g, it produces two

11 Campbell (1975) 246–9. The edition was published by G. Schirmer (1944), but based on an original scoring made unfortunately from a faulty partbook set, now GB-Lbl, Add. MSS 29410–5.
12 See Dodd (1973–4) for study of this sett.
13 Coates and Dart (1955) = MB IX, no. 80.
14 Dering, Pavan no. 4 and Mico no. 2, both in 5 parts, would have been known; though it is an older trait, as e.g. in Phillips, 'Pavana Dolorosa' a5, the ensemble setting found in GB-Lbl, Egerton MS 3665, ff. 517v–518.
15 Cf. the opening of the sett for two violins no. 7 in d, Lawes ed. Lefkowitz (1963) = MB XXI, no. 17a and Lawes ed. Pinto (1991) = MB LX, no. 15a.

110

Ex. 29: Fantasy (87)

irregularly-resolved clashes as each treble a' slides with a bright harsh-
ness over its partner's g'. The added second is repeated at bar 6 , this
time the harsher minor second interval e'–f'. As noted by Gordon
Dodd, there is a constant hankering after e-based chords and harmonies in the pieces of the sett, which serves several purposes. Related
to the motivic germ at the start of this introductory piece, it is a pivot-
point for hinting at related harmonies in a, and even b, which is rarely
strongly stated but kept behind as a permanent threat. Lawes' key-
schemes are limited when compared to some of the more extraordinary key-ranging activities of Ferrabosco II and Jenkins; but the tonal
schemes are seldom grossly unsubtle. One bears in mind the pres-
sures on a public figure to entertain at all costs, and makes the comparison with Lawes' violin setts and the Royall Consort itself, where
most of the key-schemes are considerably flatter in conception and
effect.[16]

The preludial first 18 bars of this preludial piece at any rate travel
some distance, by means of a swaying motion over a slothful semibreve movement in the basso line that broadens upwards (by way of
the theme in augmentation), as well as downwards, to a grand gesture in the dominant of the relative minor, e (bar 18). (The whole section could well be repeated, if the 'pause'-marks found in John
Browne's partbooks here imply, as often, more a point of congruence
than an outright hiatus.) A trio and quartet are left with the task

---

[16] For Ferrabosco see ed. Pinto (1990) no. 7, the 'In Nomine through all parts'; ed.
Ashbee and Bellingham (1992) = MBLXII, *passim*, and especially ed. Pinto (1992). For
Jenkins see 4-part fantasies nos. 4, 7, 15 in particular, and 5-part no. 4, pavan no. 1;
also Ashbee (1992).

respectively of exploring some of the relative key's melancholy, in an accompanied treble solo, and then of repairing back to key in anapaestic phrases reminiscent of the first strain from the five-part alman in C. At home-coming (bar 35) the significant E–F–G is stated in the bass and high e″ in the treble. A brief fugato on a contrasting downward theme (to 49), derived from the quartet, was inserted possibly more out of a need for balance than to forward any cogent organic development; but nonetheless it succeeds in returning the piece to its origins by giving over the coda to the simple anapaest in augmentation (two crotchets and a semibreve). Lines I–II hang stubbornly onto their (inverted) pedal e″, as the bass sounds out various triadic positions of the key C, all faintly epicene and hankering after the unstated keys of e and b, before reaching an accomodation between the e″–f″–g″ motif (in line II) and scalar fifth c–g (in line V). The effect of this limited play with a simply-calculated motivic row is to emphasise the preludial role of the whole piece; naturally something more has to follow.

With the second fantasy, as elsewhere, the creative dam seems to be truly breached. The initial motif's movement is from the tonic towards the significant sixth, and back away from it to the fifth, a–g, which lets through a torrent of surging quavers to ride over it and extend it to the seventh. The resulting florid expansion of the motif is an awesome display of wanton creativity; except that it is brought to a halt by a dramatic turn to the relative minor in bar 23, introduced by a sharp and querulous treble e″–f″. It brings back memories from previously, collapsing the more leisurely move to a in bars 6–18 of the first fantasy into two brief bars. (There seems to be a need for a slight rallentando, a 'drag', in bar 22 in order to let the following ten bars blossom as they should.) What it does next is another of those astonishing moments in this remarkable six-part series of pieces. Tempo seems to thicken and slow as the texture sheds its quaver values and turns stiff as a thixotropic gel. The bass begins a broad downward path, as in the first fantasy (bars 15–18), but now persists in it, straight down to C, and would-be re-establishment of the major key. The achievement is not allowed to rest more than a minim-beat, as, in one of the most subversive moves that the inner parts ever make, line III slips a b (seventh) into the chord (bar 25), that drives the fabric

112

relentlessly back to the minor again. Lines I and VI emerge out of this in canon, and carry the significant melodic strands through richly coloured dissonance. (Ernst Meyer chose this moment as *his* exemplar of Lawes at his most masterful).

At this point the piece breaks in half, signalled by pause-marks. The second section is a tribute to a predecessor, but not the teacher Coprario one might expect; and to take advantage of the pause and ask why is to show the range and distinctiveness of Lawes' achievement. If he had really been brought up to look to Coprario for guidance in composing fantasies, then little help through example would have been available in the six-part field. The eight surviving six-part pieces by Coprario are all very much in the vocal idiom, and almost certainly originated as texted pieces. They are in vocal scorings, chiefly 2Tr–A–2T–B (allowing for a little variation in the inner lines that can make IV into another Alto, or V into a Baritone). One calls them texted pieces rather than madrigals owing to their ambivalent relation to the Italian texts, where these survive. Two are untitled; of the others only two have surviving text-underlay. (As it comes to us, this underlay is far from idiomatically fitted to the music, hardly surprising in the case of copyists struggling with a foreign language.) Had Lawes been constrained by a pupil–master relationship, one would expect more tokens of acknowledgement in the six-part works, let alone the five-parters; but all the signs are that the gallimaufry jammed together by Coprario in those chamber 'fantasies' of his exerted little influence when Lawes came up against real problems of hammering out structures. Instead, Lawes showed his respects to an equally exalted but remoter figure, that of the father of the Jacobean fantasy, Alfonso Ferrabosco II.

After the luxuriant summation of the fantasy's first section, a surprisingly meek, unassuming position is given to the entry that begins the second strain after the pause-bar; seven notes reiterated on the significant e' over a mobile bass that rises through the octave. The key in which this repeated-note theme occurs most often in Lawes is his C (major), or, in the violin works in general, *D*, and its stridency and persistence answer to the key's virile, even warlike, qualities. It recalls, however indirectly, the repetitive rhythm and pitch used to express conflict in Monteverdi's *stile concitato*. It makes in this instance

113

a combination with an unmistakable borrowing from Ferrabosco's best-known six-part fantasy, no. 2 in c–C. This piece was widely copied and must have been known to Lawes since he wrote it out into the Shirley books, where White's six-part fantasy no. 2 was also included. Surviving copies in fact show the piece to have been the most popular, if not most profound, of all Ferrabosco's six-part fantasies.[17]

Like so many of them, in four or six parts, it falls into two halves, the overlap of which is usually crudely concealed. In this piece, no pretence at disguise at all is laid on; one self-aware source even describes it as a piece of '2 Strains'. The thematic material of its first, minor, half is worked right up to the double bar without needing one of Ferrabosco's customary pedal points to signal its imminent end, since the notated break between the sections performs that duty. It is the second part that struck Lawes as worthy of consideration. Though the key-signature of Ferrabosco's model is a modal one flat, from start to finish, the first half flips this into the minor outright by incidental flats, while the second approximates to the major by sharpening (or naturalising) the b flats of the signature whenever needed. Lawes deepens the force of Ferrabosco's theme, also one of seven notes, by omitting the otiose quaver frills, which enables him to spend longer on the prominent e'. The main difference is in the harmonic plan. Ferrabosco's is an uncomplicated tonic–dominant alternation, which stresses the complete triads on both these degrees of the scale. The total effect is unsubtle: transparent and light, which obviously suited late Jacobean amateur taste admirably. Lawes makes the ambiguous third of the scale (e) the pivot, giving ready access to the relative minor as well as the degrees open to Ferrabosco. Five bars suffice to turn it round from this minor to a statement of the major triad that parallels Ferrabosco's opening; by which time the economy of Lawes' reconsideration is apparent. He merges both parts of Ferrabosco's 'cell', the repeated notes and the quaver runs in the bass beneath, and holds aloft the obstinate high e" through thick and thin (such as through clear implications of G in bar 39: Ex. 30a–c). The

---

[17] Musical texts in Ferrabosco ed. Pinto (1990), no. 2, and Coates and Dart (1955) = *MB* IX, no. 78.

Ex. 30a: Fantasy no. 2 a6   Alfonso Ferrabosco II

Ex. 30b: Ibid

underlying bass part is also a fulfilment of the scalar fifth as first
heard in the opening and closing bars of Fantasy one.

Unlike Ferrabosco, Lawes can hardly be bothered to indulge in
augmented statements of the theme, but instead lets its natural forward momentum infect all the parts from bar 42 on with a quaver
eagerness to arrive at the trysting-point (46). By then, until the end, a
concurrent clamour of repeated-note phrases has arisen, many of them
lengthening out to double the original seven notes, and still stressing

Ex. 30c: Fantasy (88)

the third—of the dominant (line II, bars 46–8) as well as of the tonic. It is a culmination of ideas not only from the previous fantasy but even from the five-part sett in C, where repeated-note motifs constitute the last bars of the fantasy and pavan, and underlie almost everything expressed throughout the alman.

It is a measure of the high seriousness now enveloping the enterprise that Lawes could feel happy in putting such an abstract alman to follow these fantasies; if alman this 'aire' is, in the nearly entire absence of typical rhythmic elements, and in view of the piece's extraordinary length (two strains of at least 30 semibreves each). One can cavil at the lack of metric variety in the fantasy repertoire for five to six parts: the absence of triple-time sections in fantasies, or for that matter triple-time pieces at all, let alone danceable dances in any metre. Lawes does not offer them, but he may be attempting to evade altogether the usual types of dance-rhythm in this massive piece (is it significant that in his organbook he first put the title 'Fantazy' to it?). The most salient features are pulse and rhythm. Initial entries make a play, in a way that is clear by bar 4, of setting up against one another two triads, Tr–T–T and Tr–B–B. With one regular entry per duple bar, this emphasises a long arching phrase that implies triple-unit bars of 3/1 (Ex. 31). The piece bars out perfectly to the final cadence in these

Ex. 31: Aire (89)

large 'bars', and most significant cadences resolve in coincidence—first bass move into a two-flat key-area at bar 10, first general cadence at 13, similar major cadence in strain two at bar 52, are all at the start of large triple movements. The rhythmic preoccupations of the five-part alman in C are enlarged upon: the anapaest two-quaver crotchet unit of the first five-part strain becomes a longer quaver figure, more like one of the jigging alleluias that both William and Henry were fond of in their psalm-settings; it also occurs in a high concentration in the Royall Consort almans in C, nos. 51–2. In strain two the same thing is given a downward (homecoming) turn, punctuated by two returns of the anapaest figure in the top parts. The main, very extended flowing figure of this second strain, first heard in treble II bar 36, has its own triple implications, as can be seen by observing the canon (fairly strictly drawn for Lawes) between bars 37 and 43–4 (Ex. 32). These downward-spiralling lines are a relief of tension from

Ex. 32: Aire (89)

the grandeur of the foregoing pieces: the sort of parlour-piece designed to show the relaxations of royalty, perhaps?—but which, like
royalty at play in public, retains an unbending composure, distanc-
ing itself from onlookers. Despite the sinuous quavers of the second
strain, the piece has a lack of momentum or strophic feel, an opacity
that puts it outside real dance repertoire; like some other aires by
Lawes that avoid categorisation, it is the sort of white elephant that
probably could occupy no niche in space–time than the one which it
permanently now inhabits.

Consort Sett VIII

The germ of the first fantasy–alman pair in the pastoral sett in F is
clear from the aire, (no. 91), which opens with the rising triadic phrase
that has given the fantasy its very apt modern nickname of 'Sunrise'
(fathered unblushingly by Layton Ring). There is a close correspondence with an alman, unassignable to any known occasion, by Lawes'
contemporary Charles Coleman (Ex. 33a–b). As usual, comparison
points up the strength of Lawes' handling. One can even detect a
certain rivalry in the process, since the six-part aires by Lawes do not
otherwise seem to have any pre-existent smaller-scale forms, or close
thematic relationship with works outside his own consort setts. (It

Ex. 33a: Alman (216)   Charles Coleman

Ex. 33b: Aire (91)

occurs elsewhere too: a sprightly alman in Lawes' sixth sett for one violin, aire no. 130, has a correspondence with Coleman's aire no. 264 too large for chance: Ex. 34a–b.) Where Coleman hangs fire, Lawes pushes through with panache. His pieces in this sett in *F* in general have one fingerprint that is plastered all over the second strain of the first aire: the clusters of repeated-note anapaests, two-quaver–crotchet, that in other less bucolic contexts are laid on less thickly (one can suspect here a musical signature to the rhythm 'William Lawes', possibly?). Another feature made much of in similar positions in the fantasy is the short downward crotchet phrase, typically b (flat)–a–g, or c–b–a with the implication of the dominant seventh on the second note: another strongly emphasised harmony throughout the sett. The composer's autograph score in fact prefaces both the two aires of this

Ex. 34a: Alman (264)   Charles Coleman

Ex. 34b: Aire (130)

sett before the fantasies: the order, though, in his two other surviving
playing parts (organ and bass viol I) differs. It is hard to believe that
he did not mentally conceive of the sett as beginning with the morn-
ing mists of the first fantasy's opening bars.

The first fantasy in F (no. 90) is formally unusual in having such
clearly defined balancing wings to it; one hesitates to fasten on it
that overworked term 'triptych', if only because the purpose and
extent of the central panel of the piece are debatable. It could merely
consist of bars 22–35; it could, though, be redefined to involve the
transitional section 36–51, which then would detract length and stature from the winding-down process in the final wing, reducing it to
the bare 12 bars before the end. Doing so, it would redefine the sym-
metry of first and last sections, if only because the festoons of quavers

in bars 36–51 read like an extended solution to the slighter synco-
pated end to the first section at bars 16–20, and therefore are more
naturally heard as part of the balancing answer to the 'sunrise'. Perhaps the visual image of triptych cannot help but miss out the dyna-
mism of the process, and one ends up by diminishing the value of
these sections individually; since, viewed statically, merely for its
dancy 'William Lawes' anapaestic rhythms, the central plateau has
no imposing presence as an altarpiece should, nor a function other
than to articulate the two wings.

The first few bars of the piece show the workshop door ajar in a
revealing way. In score Lawes, composing more and more off the top
of his head as the six-part setts wended their way, began with the
first entry of the tenor (line IV) an octave lower. The necessity of inserting an unshapely single-note F in line V to give the tenor a floor,
which then forced the bass to forestall its own imitative entry, was
soon seen as a blemish; but led only to a make-shift solution, hoick-
ing the tenor up by an octave to double the alto line at pitch (Ex. 35).
This forces an awkward leap back, in bar 4 of the amended tenor, one
of those little sutures that without pre-knowledge are barely

Ex. 35: Fantasy (90)

121

detectable. It also says something of Lawes' attitude to his tenor lines. In the six-part texture the dual function of doubled trebles and basses is clear enough. The alto is the shape-shifter of the texture, often abetting the tenor to make a third pair, but as like as not to function as an internal comment or descant on the treble lines, in the upper part of its register. In the impressionistic haze of these opening bars it is deliberately unclear which part is intended to be dominant; the alto pre-empts treble I's regular imitation by a single minim, off-pulse, intertwining itself like decorative acanthus around the uppermost contour.

Another textural difficulty is situated in the last part of the opening section on the triadic 'sunrise' theme, after bar 16; it resembles closely Lawes' peremptory expedient of cutting down to size the opening of the five-part fantasy in C, when the rate of increase in its momentum began to seem to him to be misjudged. He there solved the problem merely by halving note-values. The same magic wand is waved here, from the second part of bar 16 where quaver runs in lines IV–VI infect the texture and bring on an attack of thick stretto

Ex. 36: Fantasy (90)

up to bar 20, all three pairs in a close approximation to canon (Ex. 36). It would hardly be worth the mention except for the curious but true fact that just this self-same Bechers Brook in the course towards the cadence is the point where players without pre-knowledge of the terrain tend to fall out of the ensemble; and for the (possibly allied) fact that when Lawes wrote out the organ part, he himself took his hands off the reins and mislaid two minim-beats in the right hand of bars 19–20. The identity between F and pastoral is one of those assumptions easily made and hard to support, and so other occurrences of the interlocking thirds, as at bars 17–20, in a context of stretto (though not pure F tonality) deserve a mention. Something similar occurs close to the beginning of Orlando Gibbons' fantasy no. 2 a6, and Gibbons elsewhere showed an affinity with this teasing and canonic way of texture-spinning, as in his three-part published fantasy no. 2.[18] There is also a correspondence with Luca Marenzio's setting of stanza one from Jacopo Sannazaro's canzona, 'Valli riposte e sole', which invokes pastoral landscapes at its opening (Ex. 37).[19]

Of the second aire little needs to be said except that it is in its general deportment a welcome return to pure alman (and consequently barred in modern editions as such, in four-crotchet units). The pointed but reposeful dominant-seventh chord, involving b flat, returns at every main cadence: at bars 2, 12, 25, positioned each time in the tenor register, and indirectly highlighting the importance for the piece of its pervasive swaying dotted rhythms. This dotted-crotchet–quaver figure takes over the second strain completely, and might have risked losing the alman's rhythmic solidity but for Lawes' teasing use of false anacruses. The first crotchet of the whole strain, in bar 13, was off-putting enough to the original users of one set of partbooks that they mistakenly took it for a confusingly notated genuine anacrusis, and proceeded to insert barlines into the next few bars

---

[18] Gibbons a6 no. 2 is in fact Meyer no. 1 and listed first in Dodd (1980–92); it is put in second place by published editions: Gibbons ed. Hobbs (1982) and ed. Harper (1982) = *MB* XLVIII; the first without score, the second without playing parts.
[19] Marenzio (1588), no. 12. This piece of course is not claimed as a direct precursor of Lawes, though the lesser-known collection of the master from which it comes was known and appreciated in England. The piece was copied into John Baldwin's MS, now GB-Lbl, RM 24.d.2, ff. 11v–12v.

Luca Marenzio

De - ser - te piag - gie a-pri-che, De - ser - te piaggie a - pri -che

a crotchet-beat out—the same disorientation is apt to be felt today, unless the tempo of the dance as a whole is kept steady and not forced. It is the combination of these seeming anacruses, placed on every succeeding crotchet beat (bars 13–14, 16 last crotchet–19, 21 last crotchet–23) that thicken and homogenise the texture; an attempt at a similar trick is carried out briefly for four bars in the second strain of Royall Consort aire no. 30, in *D*.

The second fantasy, as so often, works a canvas with freer brush-strokes than in the first: the effect is of greater length, simply because Lawes possessed the trick of creating his tempo as he goes along, solidifying or thinning out the wash of incidental detail. The first half of the theme in four innocuous notes introduces a very potent rise from fifth to sixth, or tonic to supertonic, that soon brings disso-nant resolutions, or other incidents in its train (such as bar 3, upward resolution of a discord in line III). The significant three-note descend-ing phrase e flat–d–c is concealed in the inconclusive tail-half of the subject, and its dominant-seventh feel is apparent in the first 20 bars up to the section end, or even thereafter; it has the effect of dragging down with it the tonal reply (b flat–a–g) into further flat keys. The two halves of the theme juxtaposed give an opportunity to indulge in much, strictly gratuitous, dissonance, as at bar 8 where the trebles create glancing seconds, between each other and also against the lowest line present. As often with Lawes' dissonance it is fleeting, but far from random; tending to introduce added tones on the second, sixth or fourth in close anticipation of a harmonic shift into related key-centres. After another strong seventh which brings to an end at bar 20 this inconclusive wandering, there is another central plateau as in the first fantasy, also on springy dance-rhythms (though these peter out within seven bars), and also leading by natural development into what loosely could be called a final section.

Here begins a winning streak, a sequence that contain some of Lawes' richest and most self-assured six-part writing, achieved in part by making full use of the organ's capabilities in accompanying selected groups of the ensemble and generally firming up the texture. The fading anapaests are succeeded (bar 28) by a marvellous organic growth from the ground up as basses initiate a duet, on the simplest of upbeat motifs, quickly turned into a quartet by the tenor lines and then into shifting quintets which have all the weight of full six-part counterpoint (by 32). The following expansion of this, loosely worked but allusive to much that has gone before, indulges in extensive 'skipping division', as then termed: arpeggiated motifs, carefully interlarded with quaver runs that hark back to the 'sunset' of the first fantasy. There is an attempt at repetition: bars 36–9 equalling 44–6 with interchange of parts in all three pairs of instruments; a happy idea, novel for Lawes, or at least unattempted before, and perhaps put in his mind by the formality of the 'wings' in the 'Sunrise' fantasy. It soon runs aground in very choppy water. Metre goes to pot under the formal strain, and all the parts dissolve into quavers, in bar 46, especially the basses who plunge down with some unorthodox fifths (carefully inserted, since not present at first scoring). The presence of a double bar here, after these motions have run their course, is editorial, but pause-marks are original. There is a good possibility that 'pause' does not mean pause in this context, but that the marks are used as signs of congruence, and indicate not a dramatic hiatus but a gradual slowing down, 'drag' in the contemporary term, until the tempo of the final epiphany is established in bar 47. Here the tonic minor, that was neglected both early in the fantasy and (for that matter) throughout the so far unbroken good weather of this sett, comes back like the 'return of the repressed', until dismissed with a final regal (if retorted) gesture in line I. This commanding phrase seems to need an augmented interval, d" flat–e "(natural), in order to work the 'open sesame' and re-establish the major key (one says 'seems', simply because original notation is ambiguous; but an e" flat would surely be out of keeping five notes from the piece's end). The sett as a whole is the gracious high summer for the whole six-part sequence; whereafter the decline to autumn and impending cold is swift and assured.

Consort Sett IX

The fantasy in B flat in many respects is a retreat from the confidence, the full idiomatic use of the instruments and liberated structure of the preceding F sett. It seems likely that the correspondence in key (C, F, B flat) between the later setts of the Royall Consort and the viol setts cannot be coincidental; and yet the difference in mood in the respective B flat setts is marked. Both seem to be imbued with much of the pastoral of the setts in F. At the same time they show wide variation in their vitality: from a suburban bustle in the almans of the Royall Consort, to the almost holiday laze of the six-part viol fantasy. (The relatively remote key of B flat also seems to inhibit Lawes in making recourse to related tonal centres, compared to his F; the contrasts that are made are the more deliberate for it.)

The general pattern of the piece, a contrapuntal introduction followed by contrasting, thinly scored airy trios and then varying attempts at summation, had been evident some years earlier, towards the end of the Jacobean development: in the few six-part fantasies by Charles Coleman, for example. In comparison there is nothing new in Lawes' structure, and it seems more like a reversion to the standards of his predecessors, where a piece is made up of an accretion of isolated sections rather than possessing any narrative continuity specific to it. The only especially characteristic episode in the piece follows the trio sections, where all the parts burst in (bars 39–40) to express a brief disparagement of progress hitherto; beginning high, but winding down in a crotchety exasperation that derives from figures of the trios. It is oddly reminiscent of the second part of a five-part fantasy by Jenkins in *B* flat (no. 6 as published). The modern specialist in the field has speculated whether its uncharacteristic harmonic flow and 'mundane' subject (certainly, ill-formed to sustain the development through which Jenkins put it) show an attempt by the composer to meet Coprario or Lawes on their territory; the piece appears to come late in his general five-part series.[20] It could also be wondered aloud if the flow of influences was a mutual one. Techniques of sustaining a whole piece through the drama of its counterpoint alone were beyond Lawes. The skills that Jenkins learned from Ferrabosco II, and used so magnificently to underpin an organic contrapuntal structure, by means like augmentation at key points, do not seem to have struck Lawes as generally worthwhile. One recalls the remark of his teacher Coprario, in his MS treatise on composition, claiming glibly that conventional means of constructing thematic material were played out, and that the modern composer was driven to 'double fuge' for the sake of novelty.

This fashion of maintayning of double fuges is most usd of Excellent authors, for in single fuges there can no such great art be shewed, but onlie in the invention thereof: Besides there hath so many bene made alreadie, as that hardlie one shall invente a single reporte to be easilie, and sweetlie brought in, butt it hath alreadie bene invented before'.[21]

The mighty successes of Jenkins in devising monothematic works on the scale of 5–6 parts, with a warmth and imagination unparalleled before or after, must in that light have seemed either impossible to rival or even (curious thought) wrong-headed for a 'modern' composer to be attempting; and indeed, any thinking contemporary in the year 1640 would have considered Jenkins past his peak, without foreknowledge of the way in which ranks were to be thinned by the

---

[20] Jenkins ed. Nicholson (1971), no. 6; Ashbee (1992), 253–4. The chief set of parts for the piece, GB-Lbl, Add. MS 30487, describes it as in 'B my key' (*B* flat).
[21] Coprario ed. Bukofzer (1952), f. 40.

coming war, the scope for composition drastically altered for good, and also of the remarkable second wind that built a new reputation for Jenkins, wider even than his old.[22]

There are some features of Lawes' *B* flat Fantasy that hint at temporary loss of direction, quite possibly resulting from an understandable inhibition after considering the example of Jenkins. Without being in any way contrapuntal, the second trio section conceals within it the opening theme, disguised by its situation in the tenor part (Ex. 38). What purpose it serves is hard to tell. The same is true of the mainly chordal section that follows the interjection, where a

Ex. 38: Fantasy (94)

sense of direction is oddly absent, owing to textural variations (of a sort that obscure the purpose behind the comparable five-part fantasy in *B* flat by Jenkins too): inconclusive chromatics in line I bar 43, line VI bars 44–5, and another passage of plummy scoring to match the opening point. Here the writing is oddly loaded: all six voices weigh in, but while chewing this rich cud sound less contrapuntal and more like naive accompanied tune than usual. The final section of the piece seems to arise from a need to enfold and justify the preceding diverse textures and their juxtapositions, since it is so obviously related to, and intended to balance graciously, the gracious opening point in its first segment. It launches on uncommonly beautiful and exactly imitative descending scales of bell-peal lineage,

---

[22] Abbey (1984) details a list for the year 1640, putting Jenkins prematurely into third place, behind the Lawes brothers.

128

bedded on a restful pedal. This bell-imitation is a souvenir of Jenkins-country, one could say was even the *spécialité de sa région*, from the number of occurrences in his pavans and fantasies.[23] The correspondences between the two are just great enough to give an inkling that Lawes must have felt a new, if transient (or even counterproductive), urge to bind together his pieces more systematically, and that the self-conscious attitude detectable throughout the piece was the result.

The caution persists in the accompanying pieces to the extent that they are bound close to the fantasy and each other by reliance on very similar scalar motifs (as, contrariwise, Jenkins had turned to disjunct themes at the beginning of the comparable *B* flat work). The aire is another massive and unwieldy beast that moves in un-dance-like way in its opening scalar point; all parts brought in smartly at minim intervals, reckless of the harsh seconds that arise in the tenor lines on both their third and fourth notes, before they have even established a presence. It is saved by the relative brevity of the first strain (8 bars), the greater concision that brevity enforces in making shifts in key, and the well-articulated treble antiphony in strain two. Rather than the 'William Lawes' anapaests, it is a dotted version with a slight swagger to it that predominates here and elsewhere in the sett, but most noticeably in the aire, bars 3–6 and 16–20; a refreshing return to suburban gaiety after the enervated repose of the fantasy.

The In Nomine, however, is the gem of the sett, and one of the high points of the whole genre; this despite the solecism in Lawes' wanton distortion of the plainsong cantus firmus. Throughout the long life of the In Nomine, from its beginnings in the late 1520s as a vocal Mass-excerpt up to the last examples, written with antiquarian zeal by the young Henry Purcell around or shortly before 1680, the cantus firmus was adapted in various ways: its durational unit changed *ad libitum* to any standard note-value, even of five beats in examples by Parsley, Strogers and Tye. (Alfonso Ferrabosco II in his 'In Nomine through all parts' freed it from any uniform value and distributed it to each of the six parts in turn, in his attempt to conceal

---

[23] 5-part pavan no. 2, last strain, bars 30–5; fantasy no. 16, bars 47–end; 6-part pavan no. 2, bars 46–50 (cf. also the 'real' bells in pavan no.1, 'The Bell Pavan', bars 29–36); fantasy no. 10, bars 46–53; no. 12, bars 39–end.

it; disguised at times even from the players themselves, perhaps.) Its pitch-level was altered to suit any instrumental tessitura, and the freely composed parts around it subjected to any whim. All along the plainsong stayed remarkably unchanged, even if composers did often omit or lengthen certain units out of its 56-breve length, often more from ignorance of the original, no doubt, than any desire to kick against the pricks. The number of pitches at which the plainsong is found are also limited, out of a certain respect too: *d* and *g* predominate, *c* and *a* some way behind. Seemingly, no-one except Ferrabosco II, for one episode in his 'Fantasy through all the parts', transposed the plainsong into *e* ; apart, that is, from Jenkins in the second of his six-part In Nomines (though an anonymous six-part example sometimes attributed to Dering does it too). That in itself is unusual enough to give another reason for suspecting a common programme with Lawes, a joint shaping of some part of their six-part outputs; for certainly one thing dared by Lawes, alone among composers, was to alter the mode of the plainsong itself; from Dorian-minor to plain major. It is not unknown to find the *accompanying* parts in predominantly major mode, as in the one surviving example by the Elizabethan, (Robert?) Goldar; but that hardly goes to these literally cavalier lengths. The jape alters most (about six sevenths) of the intervallic relations between successive notes.[24]

Lawes' version of the plainsong is fairly pure, omitting only three notes from the repeated final four, and otherwise extending three others by a breve or three (two notes are altered in pitch-level: bar 29 a third too low, and 41 a tone too high; which are relatively small matters). It suggests a wilfulness about the procedure, especially since the plainsong is nailed so conspicuously to the treble masthea; like the version in *e* by Jenkins in fact. (This piece did attract one imitation of minor musical significance, of which more in the next chapter.)

Prose exposition is useless against a piece like this, in which all the resources have combined under favourable auspices and deliver a smooth and faultless passage. This time the scales are downwards,

---

[24] Goldar's piece in Doe (1988) = *MB* XLV, no. 134. Goldar (or Golder) was one of the Windsor organists; his will is dated 28 Nov. 1563.

except for those reversed to provide contrast in the middle high quartet (bars 29–35), and the following bass dialogue (36–42 or so). Unlike (say) the second fantasy in *F*, where the same control over the forces is exhibited, the movement throughout the piece is constant and unaltering. The quavers that begin to sprout by bar 13, and preen through the texture like a butterfly emergent from the cocoon, all have the same unhurried air, no matter how extremely figurate the division-figures they cut against the background glow. The momentum is irresistible once begun. Lawes found himself compelled at an early stage of work to reshape extensively the middle quartet, from one of much slower note-values into the present shimmering quaver free-canon; to that extent the piece itself had taken over in shaping its unique destiny. There are also signs in his score that enthusiasm for florid motion outran for a time his own better sense of pace. Line V in bars 16–17, and I and V in bar 53 contain some extra divisions inserted over calmer versions; but it was in the end the simpler lines that were later allowed to circulate in preference to the florid, no doubt rightly—the florid line V in bar 16 is betrayed by this enthusiasm for further figuration into very audible consecutive fifteenths with line I.[25] The final cadence, like so much else here, is matched very distinctly with those in the two preceding pieces, with the signal grace of an added sixth in the penultimate chord. It is the final moment of Indian summer before the very chill breath that clouds the end to the whole series with the threat of winter to come.

Consort Sett X

The sett in *c* brings with it as many unsolved mysteries as its outright stature in the class of great chamber music of all time deserves to handle. Textually, it shows the fewest signs of revision, which by paradoxical contraries is a sign of a certain incompletion. Indications elsewhere of reworking stand out here and there in the composer's scorebook, and are valuable indications of working methods, of how

[25] The figurate version is printed in preference to the simpler in Lawes ed. Lefkowitz (1963), no. 5.

Lawes sometimes had to correct his structure in several respects before feeling satisfied. The problems of the two earliest five-part pieces in *g* had been resolved by the time of scoring; but almost immediately the blue pencil is seen at work, as Lawes excised a section from the first fantasy in *a*—his method was usually of hacking out the dead wood, and seldom of being compelled to bolster thin material. Where dissatisfaction with scoring in five parts resurfaced in the later sett in *F*, it was the inner parts for the dances that needed readjustment. The fantasy in *C* underwent not the trauma of outright excision, but a shot of adrenalin through halving of its note-values in the opening point. In the earlier setts a6 the main fine-tuning was in reducing efflorescent detail. The agitated texture of the fantasy in *g*, bars 36–9, evidently seemed confused and in need of simplification; the too-exuberant lines in fantasy no. 2 in *C* had to be cut back in bars 8, 13 and 17. The sett in *F* a6 is the most stable textually, bar an adjustment to texture in the first four bars of fantasy one, though a few bars later (16–20) it was the the rate of progress, as in the five-part fantasy in *C*, that brought on some tampering with the sluggish bars. In the *B* flat sett there is similar (not very substantial) wavering over the shaping of phrases, either by cutting out excrescences, or for that matter pondering whether to add them. All through, though, a continuous engagement, patting into place detail on a quite minor level, is plain.

The lack of adjustments in the sett in *c* could of course mean that the composer had reached a new impressive level of certainty, and the sett as a whole to a large part seems to bear this out in its grand sweep (it received the accolade of being the only six-part sett excerpted entire, as representative of Lawes' achievement, in *Musica Britannica*). A few details do, however, crop up to suggest that time was running out for the composer for whatever reason, and that further revision might have taken place under the right circumstances. For a start, Lawes for once did not write his own organ part to the first fantasy and the start of the second (bars 1–23). The hand which helped him out was unwilling to take on the responsibility of creating a semi-independent part after Lawes' inimitable practice, or else unused to the idea.[26] As a result these parts do nothing further than make a short-score intabulation of the pre-existing strings, and indulge in some unusually cumbersome stretches and note-clusters, that exceed the unmanageability of the composer's own lumpy but very effective way with chamber-organ texture.

Any distance further from Lawes than necessary is especially to be regretted in this first fantasy, owing to its remarkable theme and its origins. It seems to be unique for the fantasy repertoire in being founded thematically on a separate vocal work by its own composer. This theme, heard first in line VI, would anyway be out of the ordinary for its contortions. The vocal piece in question is a setting of a prose paraphrase from the penitential Psalm 6, verses 6–7 and 4–5, textually seemingly unrelated to any standard poetic version, and possibly 'set' as a task by some influential person for Lawes to put to music (Ex. 39a–b). The same (royal?) influence may have been brought to bear on him to ensure a fantasy on the same theme: apparently unsingable, though it is not so wayward as first sight suggests (the first seven notes it hits have a strong resemblance to the first five in the theme of the *Musical Offering*). It had been only a fleeting initial statement, for bass voice alone, in the psalm-setting, and then abandoned without further ado. Here Lawes does not give it especially extended or contrapuntal treatment (bars 1–21), and even as it stands it is developed in very malleable forms, succeeded by bar 15 by a passage of sequential thirds quite similar to that towards the close of the five-part fantasy in *c*, bars 40–8.

The piece is simply tripartite; far from overlong, and with nothing to bind the three sections together except as stages in an internal debate, contrasted very sheerly in gait and in the types of emotion that are implied. Near-despair of the first part receives friendly reproof in the relative major steadily maintained through the second part, supplemented in the third by a naive, nursery-like chant resembling nothing so much as a hymn-tune (unidentified if such, but

[26] The hand is one of several similar scripts that belong to members of the Tomkins family: candidates for identification include John Tomkins (though he was dead in 1638, probably too early for this composition) and Giles Tomkins, the most likely, who as a keyboard player fits the bill very well. See Irving (1990) and correspondence in *M&L* lxxii (1991), 517–18.

Ex. 39a: I am weary of my groaning

I _____ am wea - ry of my groan - ing,

I am wea - ry of my groan - ing, I am

I am wea - ry of my groan - ing, I am wea -

I am wea - ry of my groan - ing, I am wea -

9 6 5 6 9 6

5

I am wea-ry of my groan-ing, my beau- ty is gone for ve- ry

wea - - ry of my groan- ing, groan - ing; my beau - ty is

- ry of my groan - ing, my beauty is gone

3 4

Ex. 39b: Fantasy (97)

134

strongly reminiscent of 'Onward, Christian soldiers'). This chant must by its position stand for otherworldly aspirations, if the initial quotation has any meaning. If so, the aspiring chromatic ascent of the third section and its coda, shared out between the trebles until it falls back at high b″ flat having failed its object, betoken the failure of orthodox pieties to resolve the problem. 'My words flye up, my thoughts remain below, / Words without thoughts, never to Heaven go'—in the words from another court and another time; from a king, Claudius of Denmark, with much on his conscience at time of prayers.

The second fantasy reads like the fruition of everything that has gone before. It is half as long again as the preceding fantasy, and in fact just beaten in length by the fantasy in *B* flat; yet it traverses a range of action at an altitude above the meanders of the longer piece. One reason is simply the management of pace, and the controlled suspense that is engendered through it. From the start there is a very even and constant current, as though one has just swung into the main stream from a tributary. It relies on the even-handed distribution of quaver movement in every phrase, and its subtle increase to round out and define the periods. With this blest handling of phrases there is hardly any need for tight thematic linkage to make the points work smoothly, though of course there is the usual family resemblance involving falls to the fifth through the submediant (the darkly stressed a flat, in this case). Throughout the whole of the sett the distinguishing tone of the themes is set by their initial falls, from the high g to the lower one. There also develops a running competition for these high places, especially in the trebles, which has not been there to the same extent before.

Lawes was, or became, a master of texture, in particular for his handling of the equivocal two-treble duet, which has an unsteady history in fantasy as well as in dance. The scope of the Jacobean six-part fantasy was set probably through the example of Ferrabosco II who, after some experimentation of his own, settled on the scoring of three equal and crossing pairs of parts as an optimum. Given the quasi-vocal limitations on part-range, set up by convention (and possibly reinforced by the need for idiomatic writing to suit the instruments' sonorities, rather than the inability of players to hit the high notes), it brought with it a perpetual problem over what to do with

135

the uninvolved parts in the contrapuntal fabric. It applies to none of them more perceptibly than the highly prominent trebles. There is an obvious preference felt by Ferrabosco to keep the parts in play as much as possible rather than diminish textures, except where contrasting choirs of high and low, in the new *concertante* way that he was happy to accomodate. It resulted, though, in a continuum of sound, filled out by the ready alternation of parts within their own band, but presenting an aural experience difficult to interpret for anyone unversed in the protocol. (The late reaction of the North family members cited earlier cannot have been untypical).

The problem is not so urgent in the four-part repertoire where (historically speaking) the fantasy began, and where a continuous texture is actually needed to maintain full harmony; nor in five parts, where the diverse textures of the madrigalian example gave stock, pre-learned excuses even to its less competent handlers. In six parts it stayed a problem, since there the contrapuntal texture has fewer easy procedures to fall back on, and must make its every move self-evidently clear. Ferrabosco never quite cracked this problem, or even perceived it; which demarcates perhaps a predecessor of the true baroque from those who saw its full dawning. Much of the same is true of the great successor in Ferrabosco's mould, John Jenkins, the subtlest shaper of individual contrapuntal lines of them all, who was also happy to inhabit the six-part plenum of fulfilled desires, like an anticipation of that state where there is no having or holding, and full individuality is left behind. Unwanted parts are simply manipulated in the direction of an unfilled part of the texture, even if in the case of the treble parts that involves shoving them upstairs to the aurally disorienting register at the top of the treble clef, d"–g" and above.

Lawes' instinctively responsive treble dialogues were in evidence from the start of his consort adventure, and spared no line or part of a line if it was later found to have made an inept contribution. In them you could therefore see a new realism. His partial return to the 'continuum' effect in the last sett could be read, not as a recantation (since the trebles do not stop their well-spaced collaborative efforts, especially as a new upward movement emerges out of the opening point around bar 13), but as a return to imbibed habits of thinking, a form of grace under pressure (a pressure which implies shortage of time). After quitting their initial high entry notes, there is in the treble parts a constant surge, a lingering on high g"s and an aspiring (even if constantly thwarted) to c''', the top of the register, that has not been heard before. The trebles had made occasional recourse to this tessitura from the start of the five-part pieces, but not to inhabit it as main territory. From this point too a new urgency infects the alto part, which finds new pastures in the top of its register, above g'.

Following the pause that ends the first section, the middle trios (Tr–B–B and Tr–T–T) can usefully be compared once again with Coleman, in his six-part fantasy no. 1 in c. For once, Coleman's considerable elegance comes off well, since his trios (both Tr–T–B) are well-poised in comparison with those of Lawes (Ex. 40). The passages in Lawes do not fit too well into breve barring; but then almanlike semibreve barring fits just as badly, since the second trio barges in, overlapping a semibreve pulse by a minim beat. Probably the wrong-footing begins at the very start of the first trio, and one should consider its first minim's-worth as an anacrusis (see Ex. 41 for a rebarred first trio, giving it as a result an anomalous final bar). The point sounds a little pedantic, but it shows just how early and precisely Lawes prepared the ground for the second trio to come in with fresh momentum, and even further ahead to bring in with exactitude the re-entry of the basses, followed by treble, in bar 35. Once more he anticipates the phrase-ending by a minim and deftly keeps the balloon in the air with a turn to the uplifting major tonality of an implied E flat—and a new significant motif in VI, then I, in bars 40–1. This wavers and cedes before some marvellously full florid writing in all voices (44–52), and then the last return of the initial motif as sequential rhythm in the final summing-up (52–8). One would think (and be wrong) that this exhausts the potential for further comment; Lawes next turned to the sacred theme he had dealt with a little flippantly in the B flat tonality.

Formally the In Nomine of the sett is peculiar. Its structure stresses the paramountcy of the outer Tr–B parts, which are entrusted the plainsong in pairs, in the order V–VI, II–I, leaving the tenor parts outside the sharing of this patrimony. The cantus firmus is exceptionally stated in semibreves, for which close precedent is hard to

Ex. 40: Fantasy no. 1 a6

Charles Coleman

Ex. 41: Fantasy (98)

spot—perhaps in the three-part In Nomines by Thomas Tomkins, which could have come the way of Lawes. The second of these by Tomkins involves a bass cantus firmus, which is unique in the ensemble (though not the keyboard) repertoire, apart from this piece of Lawes', that is.[27] Lawes' cantus firmus is furthermore stated twice completely, but perversely each voice in the pair is given only one half of it. In both cases the equal parts interchange between the 30th and 31st notes, and the second of each pair adds on a coda containing a(flat)–g, which stresses the plagal endings. By these repetitions the plainsong could be considered as wellnigh in continuous variation form, which again reminds one of the keyboard repertoire.[28]

Puzzles about scoring, models and form are only a prelude to one of the weirdest In Nomines in the repertoire for its refusal to abide by norms. Thematic material, contorted to a degree that suggests deformity, has lost any attempt at exact contrapuntal replication; fragmented lines stagger against each other like the derelict shells of bombed housing. The three uppermost voices continue clinging to their new high tessitura, which by oversight or not produces some undigested detail which the composer may have been in the course of revising at the time of circulation for the whole collection. Line I bars 9 (last minim) to 10 (end) in the score originally read an octave higher, an overpowering entry that Lawes decided to expunge while still working over the page. The high line persists , however, in the organ part, possibly by oversight—and, as a consequence of the composer's second thought, in this phrase the alto part is left exposed, a third above the abased treble. Another odd detail that might have been caught on re-examination is the small string of three consecutive unisons between I and III in bar 14; for even though Lawes was not squeamish about these defects, or even flaunted them, this one seems a little prominent for comfort (the next brief parallel movement between alto and a treble, this time line II in bar 22, does not have the same feeling of transgression). Throughout there is a remote but acute atmosphere of mourning; the independent diminished fourths and irregularly resolved dissonances that Lawes always had

[27] Printed in Tomkins ed. Irving (1991) = MB LIX.
[28] Examples by John Lugge of Exeter Cathedral seem to be the closest in time, though it is hard to see any direct link.

cultivated have here a new feeling of disjointedness from their context, rather as in that other extreme of mourning as expressed by Lawes, his three-part vocal lament for John Tomkins, 'Musique, the Master'.[29] The connection remaining is through motivic rhythm, as the parts follow the occasionally aimless path of the bass-situated plainsong (which happily does linger upon contrasting key-areas, on the third, fifth and sixth degree of the scale).

Rhythm is the key to the second half of the piece also, a relentless pounding at a phrase with a repeated-crotchet head that becomes superseded by its own jingly curvetting quaver tail, a procedure repeated in the wild free ride after the treble interchange (bar 44). Francis Baines detected here in this final section the tramp of Cromwell's New Model Army, an interesting notion which must be anachronistic by several years; however, the military skirmishing in the fantasy in *d*, no. 1 from the Royall Consort, bars 33–47, is just as menacing, and possibly contemporaneous with this In Nomine. Even so one can allow in the whole of this piece an air of foreboding or prophecy that, in whatever way plucked from the air, cannot be unheeded; like Kubla Khan's 'ancestral voices, prophecying war'. Both halves of the treble section end with rearing and plunging dotted rhythms like those encountered briefly in the *B* flat In Nomine, but in a different mood, impassioned instead of sedate.

After this, the aire resembles nothing more than a desperate mustering-call. Its opening is rhythmically reminiscent of the preceding aire in *g*, and is alike in the scalar path it takes down to the dominant (bars 6–8, like aire in *g* bars 11–13). The dotted-minim and quaver scalar sequences (bars 11–16, ironed out to a rising chromatic version in bars 37–43) , recall fantasy no. 2, bars 52–8; the opening of the second strain perhaps section two of the In Nomine. Uniquely simple and spare are the canonic repeated-crotchet groups, possibly a written-out slow 'organ-shake' to be played in a single bow, over a suddenly static basso line (bars 28–34); a chordal moment of Spartan resolve, allowing the voices a breathing-space before re-entry, and the plunge back into the unquelled storm.

---

[29] W. and H. Lawes (1648), and GB-Ob MS Mus. Sch. B. 2, p. 101.

V
Close

The preceding discussion may have been a magpie progress, picking the shiniest trinkets out of a mass that cries out for more extended analysis. But as an initial trial it is not untoward: in fact the large-scale fantasy repertoire as a whole, even without the wayward but masterly input from Lawes, reads like a series of fairly unconnected stylistic ventures that each require their own approach. There is a main thread connecting the beginning of the 17th century with its end in Purcell: the thin line of the four-part repertoire. In its graded form (Tr–A–T–B) it had most pretensions to maintaining serious counterpoint; the more public repertoire in five to six parts turns up a less predictable grain when sliced, since it is compromised from the start by adoption of and reference to more transient musical fashions, especially vocal. But even in comparison with the five- and six-part works of Jenkins, Lawes seems that much less self-contained and absolute, more bound up in a process of reworking common ideas, whether he originated them on his own or borrowed from others. In public and private modes alike there was naturally a call to 'make it new'; an undoubtable imperative for any writer who attempted a fantasy to be original in the devising of, or else reshaping of someone else's, material. In the hands of the smaller craftsmen the failures can be dismal, just as the successes when they are met with are peerless. Of the two routes to this higher level, the inner produced the controlled and perfected gestures of Jenkins; the outer, the restless innovation of Lawes.

To some extent they are complementary. The prayerful hush felt so often in Jenkins' viol-consort music has no real parallel in Lawes; contrariwise, the extrovert parade of technique in the continuo-based ensemble may be something that Jenkins was driven to late in life, and found himself excelling in (possibly to his own surprise). Rather than seeing the two composers as embodying opposing abstract tendencies—such as beautiful and sublime, or classical and romantic; anachronistic terms, of which the second pair begs the question of the possibility of classicism—it is preferable to see them as

141

approaching the fantasy from differing social levels: one emphasising the skill of counterpoint as the middle-class puritan merchants, successors of the clergy, were proud to do; the other driven by the professional's obligation to entertain the well-to-do, rather than edify, and feeling no initial need of outmoded techniques to enrich his art.

From all that has become clear about chronology so far it seems that, while Jenkins in mid-career had to adapt to the new continuo forms to flourish, Lawes, for motives not overtly to be read from detail internal to the music, decided to extend his range backwards and pay greater attention to tradition. But rather than letting it go at that, as though the outmoded possessed some intrinsic value that commanded respect, it may be more fruitful to ask some questions on a more naive level and see whether the possible range of answers pins down more exactly what Lawes was trying to do in these unprecedented setts of music. When (as precisely as possible) were they written? Where were they performed? What sort of a following did they gain, and for how long?

Apart from Jenkins, it is hard to name any composer for the larger-scale ensemble known to have been writing in the 1630s, let alone after. John Hingeston's works are the only ones, as mentioned before, to take the innovation by Lawes, of combining dance-forms with fantasies in five and six parts to the organ, a bit further. There is a preponderance of smaller-scale ensembles in Hingeston's collected works, as he himself bequeathed them to the Oxford Music School; but he did write five-part setts containing the lighter corant and saraband that were too trivial to be acceptable in the company of pavans and almans while Charles was on the throne (though not at the Lord Protector's court, it seems).[1] The troubles of the century's middle years had the odd effect of turning the younger Matthew Locke back to the smaller-scale chamber works in four and fewer parts, for which organ no longer was regarded as the standard continuo. However, for these he invented particularised sequences, composed of all the dance forms known to the earlier Caroline court in large-scale form, but treated by him in miniature and exactly aligned, ensuring a watchmaker's jewelled regularity.

---

[1] Listed in Dodd (1980–92); see Hingeston ed. Dornenburg (1991–2), and Hulse (1983).

What, then, gave Lawes the impetus for ensemble music in five and six parts, at such an awkward time? It is hard to push his initial ventures into five-part fantasy back much before 1630. The early '30s seem to be the time when the Caroline court established a secure musical identity and cultivated the new dance-suite, as witnessed in the new arrays of dances by Coleman and Lawes. The decision to proceed with consort setts for the viols cannot date from much before 1636: after the Royall Consort in its primary form, and the dazzling setts for one and two violins. At this point, when so much was moving forwards, it seems strange to have to suppose that timidity or traditionalism set in. The key to what was happening was possibly not so much a failure of nerve as a sign of growing confidence, the realisation by the king's musicians that they had a formidable corporate identity.

Sir John Hawkins was the first to notice the significance of the lawsuit mounted by the king's musicians, in their capacity as a corporation within the City of Westminster, against the encroachment of the Musicians' Company.[2] A decision in Chancery of 1634 established the royal servants in their pre-existent rights to practice their art without let or hindrance from the Company of the City of London (which had had its rights granted only since 1604), and paved the way for a separate charter of 1635. This can be seen as part of the move by the administration of the 1630s to encourage weak trade organisations without royal protection to enlist under a new and (it was hoped) vigorous authority. How much success the new corporation thereafter enjoyed is not well documented, but one can expect it to have been considerable at first.[3] Charles Butler, the tiresome clergyman advocate of a new orthography, hailed its creation in the Epistle Dedicatorie to King Charles of his treatise, *The principles of musik* (1636), and paid special attention to the coat of arms granted the company by Charles' father James I, which bore as a crest 'the *Orphean Lyre*'. He expressly compared the rights granted to the constitution

---

[2] Hawkins (1776), ii, 695–8. Material reprinted in *RECM* V (1991), 245–69. Curiously or not, this affair passed Burney by.

[3] *RECM* V, 252 reprints the petition of the musicians after the restoration, claiming that their corporation had enjoyed 'some esteeme' in its pre-war state.

of the French 'Musicall Academi' under Charles IX; a parallel with resonance, if similar advances in musical art were to be expected of this new institution as of its august trans-Channel precursor.[4] The impressive array of royal servants supporting the petition of 1635 included, of course, the Lawes brothers. It is worth floating the idea that some of the fresh confidence which the chamber music of Lawes exudes around this date, the manifold experimentation with novel chamber groups, derives in part from a feeling that a new order was dawning. If the move to subsuming the disparate traditions of the viol consort repertoire under new arrays resulted from some such communal success in imposing an order upon the profession as a whole, there should be no surprise in that. Nor should there be surprise if Lawes had felt a new need to build upon past experience in looking to the future (as at this stage he undoubtedly would have, being blest with no foresight), and turned to older colleagues like Jenkins to deepen his understanding of the past. Total conjecture, of course; but something there was that spurred Lawes on, and in the absence of further evidence one must use the means to hand.

Also entirely speculative is the query about the place of original performance. The Banqueting House is all that survives today of Whitehall Palace in the 1630s. A disastrous fire on 4 January 1698 destroyed the rest utterly, and we are left with ground-plots from a survey of 1669 by Ralph Greatorex, a well-known instrument-maker, to work out what the lie of the apartments in the '30s would have been—it is not considered that much furbishment had been done in the intervening years.[5] One building on the plan is marked out as a music room, but was more likely used as a rehearsal room than for concert-giving. Ground-plans unfortunately show nothing of the upper floors where living quarters were, and where musicians of the private music undoubtedly were permitted entry to the presence

---

[4] Butler (1636), sig.¶4. It is noticeable that Butler did not dare to inflict his new orthography on the king in this epistle, unlike the remainder of the book.
[5] See Holman (1993), Pinto (1993) for discussion of the palace rooms. The best reproduction of illustrative material is in *Survey of London*, ed. Montagu H. Cox and Philip Norman, XIII (1930), XIV (1931) and XVI (1935); also *The History of the King's Works*, gen. ed. H. M. Colvin, V (1976), 264–5 and pll. 35–7, 40B.

chamber to give entertainment. If further honoured with the status of Gentleman of the 'Bedchamber', as some highly favoured soloists were, then access to royalty outside normal times would have been permitted in fulfilling their obligations. The instrumentalists of the Royall Consort (if that was a subgroup of the private music—though it seems unlikely—rather than an appellation for the musical collection itself) would actually have formed a convenient group for purposes of access: two violins with two theorbos are ideally portable, and bass viols relatively mobile too. But there is less reason to think that efforts would have been made to accommodate groups of five to six string players carting a chamber organ with them, just for the performance of a highly specialised chamber repertoire. One has also to envisage some sort of concert performance for the court at large if only to explain why and how the music circulated relatively quickly amongst amateur players, who otherwise would have little or no chance to hear the music and less reason to wish to acquire it for private use.

Evidence does exist for the use of the royal theatre, the Cockpit-in-Court, for musical evenings during the Protectorate. Oliver Cromwell entertained the entire Commons there, from afternoon (following the early dinner enjoyed in that day) until the evening of 20 February 1657, with 'rare Musick, both of Instruments and Voyces', to celebrate his deliverance from attempted assassination in the royalist Sindercombe Plot. At some other unspecified time during the Protectorate, Roger L'Estrange, younger brother to Sir Nicholas, while strolling in St. James' Park, heard sounds of an organ emanating from one of the rooms adjacent to the theatre where John Hingeston, Master of the Music, practised. Curiosity whetted, he found on entry 'a Private Company of some five or six Persons' entertaining themselves—with one of Hingeston's setts, one is tempted to suggest. They then 'desired me to take up a *Viole*, and bear a *Part*', L'Estrange, later wishing to be known as an ardent monarchist, had embarrassingly to confess; for soon after, 'In comes Cromwell; He found us Playing, and (as I remember) so he left us.'[6]

---

[6] L'Estrange (1662). See Hulse (1983), Pinto (1993), Scholes (1934), 49, 142.

Between 1633 and 1638 the theatre had been little in use for theatricals, and one is greatly tempted to suggest that, at the least, the court had a fine site available for concert-giving if one had been required, at just the time when Lawes was composing profusely. One must admittedly bear in mind the possibility that Lawes was composing principally for his fellow-musicians in the Private Music, and that it was their *esprit de corps* that sustained his output. That much is undeniable, and Lawes is unlikely to have written what he did without their approbation; but in the circumstances that hardly seems to provide the be-all and end-all of the activities of a royal servant, who was certainly expected to serve his hours of attendance and must have had high demands made on his abilities. There are few signs of how composers were rewarded, if at all, for composition as opposed to performance, and the lack of easily recognisable names that spring to mind to set beside that of Lawes does suggest that in this age, as most others, a good share of the responsibility for the creation of considerable *oeuvres* arose from the composer's own internal sources of vitality rather than from any exterior stimulus.

The Royall Consort, as well as having become absolute music, can in its own right be considered prime information about music. In the absence of other information concerning the dancing habits of courtiers in the reign of Charles I, the extent to which it provides—it *is*—the evidence for the emergence of suite-form in England can hardly be overstressed. It has been widely assumed, from the evidence of keyboard music, to which scholars have looked most readily, that the accretion of the alman–corant-saraband sequence together with following jig was a random and almost fortuitous affair. Without an array of good sources for keyboard works, it has been adjudged safest to see the establishment of the suite as dating at best from the 1650s; William Lawes himself has been denied the credit for keyboard works ascribed to him, partly because sequences found in the few surviving MSS differ in their makeup.[7] By bending over backwards it has even been possible to snatch from Lawes the *cachet* of arranging a work by Orlando Gibbons for keyboard, on the

---

[7] Cooper (1972); Caldwell (1973), 152, 155.

improbable ground that Gibbons (d. 1625) is more likely to have made the arrangement himself from a work by Lawes.[8] There is scope here for objective examination, in light of the fact that the Royall Consort and similar ensemble works from other composers were providing just the type of sequences not attested from keyboard sources for another twenty years. Why it was that this amalgamation of pieces happened then, and in England, and succeeded in becoming standard for so long, makes for a long answer.

Some part in it must be played by the changing shape of the danced revels in the late-Jacobean court, where lighter dances were ousting the old pavan–galliard pair, that had taken precedence over almans and corantos until at least the second decade of the century. King James I is not remembered for his sophisticated musical tastes; in fact it is hard to find any agreeable aspects to his character, beyond the fact that he kept a pet kingfisher. But there can be gleaned some incidental evidence that he was not boorishly averse to, and even had a nose for, good music; and his well-known passion for good dance was a further mark of his aesthetic sense. A reason for his notorious cultivation of court favourites was their dancing skills. The last and greatest of these was George Villiers, later Duke of Buckingham, whose dancing was legendary; one of the few dance-treatises of the time was dedicated to him and his wife, by the French dancing-master De Lauze in 1623.

The way in which great resentment was created through Buckingham's relentless nepotism, in bringing his indigent relatives to court after 1619 and fitting them out with sued offices and posts, is witnessed in the tittle-tattle about their country-bumpkin habits. It had apparently a direct effect upon court dance: 'because they could not learne the French Dances so soone as to be in gay Clothes, Countrey Dances must be the garb of the Court, and none else must

---

[8] Ibid. 112. The original masque dance by Gibbons is GB-Lbl, Add. MS 10444, no. 42, 'The first of the Lords', a2 Tr–B. The piece occurs further ascribed to Gibbons, in GB-Och, MS Mu., 1003, f. 3v; GB-Och 1113, p. 100, US-NYp, Drexel 5612, p. 115. The arrangement in the hand of Ben Cosyn found in F-Pc, MS Rés. 1185 from its ascription to Lawes can therefore mean only that Lawes arranged the piece for keyboard in person.

be used', according to one fairly spiteful account.[9] Country dances, as remarked by previous investigators, may mean just that: the dances of the regions rather than simple 'heys' or chain dances; so that this comment may imply that the Villiers clan was shown up as provincial, rather than socially inept or out of its class. Nevertheless, the decade of Villiers' influence over James and then the new king, Charles I, was marked by the change in fashions, possibly led by his own unsettled energies. The new 'trio-sonata' scoring entered the fantasy repertoire, in Orlando Gibbons' famed *Fantazies*; dedicated, by no coincidence, to a creature of Buckingham's, one of the mushroom growths of the day. Buckingham himself seems to have promoted the new music.

It was at this juncture, also probably by no coincidence, that the newer dances of the Continental lower orders began to spread in England. When Buckingham accompanied Charles, then Prince of Wales, in a madcap scheme to gain the hand of the Infanta of Spain in 1623, his wife wrote to him keeping him abreast of the progress of their one-year-old daughter Mall, not quite walking:

when the saraband is played shee will sett her thum and her finger to gether ofering to snape and then when tomdufe is sunge then shee will shake her a pron and when shee hears the tune of the claping dance my lady frances huberd taught the prince shee will clape both her hands to gether and on her brest.[10]

Apparently at this time the saraband was still being danced to the accompaniment of extemporised plucked strings, with castanets or small bones for percussion, and may not even then have reached totally respectability. Lute sources, like keyboard sources, are scanty for the 1630s, but it must be significant that Lord Herbert of Cherbury's Lutebook, that was added to much in this decade, contains hardly

[9] Sir Anthony Weldon, *The Court and Character of King James* (1650) 134, as quoted by J. P. Cunningham (1961); Dean Smith and Nicol (1944–5).
[10] GB-Lbl, Harleian MS 6987, ff. 119–122v; Lady Katherine Manners to George Villiers 16 July [1623], also quoted in De Lauze ed. Wildeblood (1952). For Tom Duff or Tom Dove, cf. 'Doves Figary' in Playford (1651*b*), no. 85.

any sarabands.[11] It is also probably of significance that all the sarabands in *d* included by Lawes in what has here been taken to be the nucleus of the Royall Consort exhibit some relation to the well-known *folia* bass (see Chapter II) and thus hint at an improvised or even popular stage not too far behind. If it took the best part of another decade for the dance to reach full acceptance, then this is not just to claim it was the dance of *arrivistes*. The big change at work, rather like that which led to the consort setts at the end of the '30s, may have been a fairly direct result of social engineering at the level of official policy.

One thing uniting James I and his son Charles was the unshakable belief in their divine prerogative to rule without assistance from mortal aid; a belief tempered in the case of James (and to a significant degree less in that of his maladroit son) by a canny sense of when and how to bow under pressure. This question of where to draw the line, when royal authority and customary expectations, or the often volatile demands of the varying degrees amongst the governed, came into conflict, was never of course in principle resoluble; but on the way to outright civil war it brought a series of interesting experiments in the tolerance or restriction of traditional activities. The permissibility of holiday games and Sabbath dancing was expressly stated, along with sporting recreations like archery, in James' *Book of Sports*, first published in 1618. This Charles decided to renew through reissue in 1633 as part of the process of enforcing conformity in church and state by harmonising old country customs with liturgical practices. Archbishop Laud was Charles' willing lieutenant in licensing approved pastimes, just at the time he began to instil stricter church government, through a series of visitations. Royal ambitions were naturally not restricted to the ecclesiastical courts; the king's secular agent in his policy of 'thorough', the Earl of Strafford, was viewed with increasing fear by the end of the 1630s for the lengths he was prepared to go in reforming the state as well.

The concern shown in the '30s for the maintenance of hierarchical

---

[11] See Craig-McFeely (1991) for Herbert of Cherbury. Stephen Haynes has pointed out the presence of two sarabands, added late on, in the hand associated with Herbert's servant Cuthbert Hely. Sarabands were a goodly parcel of the repertoire of amateurs by the 1630s, especially following Continental travel: Leech-Wilkinson (1993).

patterns in social life was nothing new, if one compares the Jacobean royal proclamations issued to encourage the seasonal remigration of the gentry from London to their country domains, in order to cultivate their social dues to their inferiors. The broad plan here was one that in its literary manifestation has persuasively been termed a 'reification of pastoral vision—the export of a courtly mode to the countryside in a way that imprinted royal power on the rural landscape ... that distance between the everyday life of the people and a king and church that held themselves aloof was precisely the space that Laudian sponsorship of old customs was designed to bridge'. In court art itself, the masque had been prime arena for the symbolic *rapprochement* of court and country.[12]

The place of suite-form in this process, and the time of its formulation, are not entirely trivial matters, since it does make a difference whether it was an expression of court ideals early in the 1630s, or whether it somehow coalesced as a result of changes in bourgeois taste well over a decade later. There is of course no direct sign through musical sources that the establishment of semi-regular suite-forms, which newly exploited rustic and popular elements, was a conscious part of court plans, and it would be grotesque to claim it when after all the Puritans, who certainly objected to the intrusion of regal power into church government, could be among the most enthusiastic of dancers. No gentleman who passed through the Inns of Court could consider himself socially secure without an ability to dance, and this attitude certainly persisted unchanged through the Commonwealth period.[13] All the same, the coincidence in timing is beyond sheer happenstance; and the establishment of a new autocratic order where all knew their place was certainly the royal project *par excellence*— though Charles, unlike Louis XIV to come, failed dismally in the main business of cowing the estates of the realm into a new order.

The extent of Charles' failure blunts one's awareness of how novel the experimentation of the time must have seemed. Some alert contemporaries picked up the message, easily enough, in the case of music. Dudley, 3rd Baron North wrote in a letter to his brother, 24 September 1638, 'Our modern fantasies in musick, and your Court-masking tunes

12 Marcus (1986), 16–20, 165 and *passim*.
13 See J.P. Cunningham (1965).

150

have taken up a change in aire and spirit, and are the better accepted'. (He was by the bye using the parallel to justify his own stylistic experiments in verse; but as comment on music of the later '30s it is still revealing).[14]

The time for fitting the saraband, and the jigs or country dances, into their niche in the hierarchy had come, even if extant keyboard sources of the Commonwealth period do not pick up suites from the previous decade that might show more precisely the origin of the new linkage in its context. But then, if this line of thought is fruitful, one would just as readily expect *not* to see the rapid absorption of courtly suite-form into the recreational music of the puritanical middle classes for a considerable time; which pattern, one of unconscious resistance perhaps, is just that shown by the sources. If the keyboard repertoire was no longer a principal medium for the most creative of composers, it was still a steady means of disseminating socially significant dances, such as the prized 'simphonies' from court masques.[15] In this respect the *D* order of the Royall Consort is noteworthy for the apparently incidental lighter dances nos. 34, 41 ('Morriss') that fall outside the alman–corant–saraband core, and appear to have been part of the earliest layer. In length and rhythm they are pretty well identical to others; such as a 'Jig' also in *D*, preserved by John Playford in his *Courtly Masquing Ayres* (1662) no. 116 (Dodd no. 251); and since this occurs also in a keyboard source compiled in the 1630s, it is probable that the whole group of this and four other items as transmitted by Playford belongs together in the period when suite-form in general was taking shape (Ex. 42).[16] Lawes, that is, was not trying out the suite-concept uniquely within the matrix of any one large chamber collection, but had probably already been generally applying it in the area of his more casual dance sets a2, for Tr–B.

[14] D. North (1659), as quoted in Lawes ed. Pinto (1979).
[15] See Holman (1975–6); Caldwell (1973), ch. viii; Sabol (1978), *passim*.
[16] Playford (1662), no. 116 = US-NYp, Drexel MS 5612, p. 175, untitled and unascribed. The other dances of the group are Playford (1662) nos. 112–15; an 'Ayre' (alman), 'Corant', A Morisco' in quadruple time, and 'Saraband': now in Dodd (1980–92) as nos. 246, 249–50, 248, 251. The three preceding items also in *D*, as printed by Playford, were taken from Matthew Locke's suite 'For seauerall ffreinds', nos. 20–2 and apparently stuck randomly in this small group of Lawes items.

Ex. 42: Jig (251)

Identifying the users of, and listeners to, the Royall Consort in its first decade of existence is still a matter for considerable speculation, though from its appearance among the music of Christopher Hatton III, the first Baron Hatton of Kirby, it is possible that it could have come into his hands during the civil war. His barony was an Oxford creation (and therefore disavowed by Parliament until the Restoration), given in early recognition of his loyalty in following the king to Oxford and administering the finances of the household as comptroller. There is naturally no direct evidence that any copying was done for Hatton in the bustle of the wartime court; and though his copyist has been identified, there is no certainty that he accompanied Hatton in wartime, or had even begun copying for him by then: but the possibility that the magnificent and unique divisions in the Pavan in C (no. 49) were a speciality devised to enliven the gloom of the lulls between the campaigns is alluring.

The evidence of the composer's holograph scorebooks, discussed in some detail above in the preceding chapter, suggests that the final touches to the new version of the Royall Consort were fairly contemporaneous with the later six-part setts for the viols and organ; and so much depends on finding a reasonable occasion for these, in order to set the whole sweep of Lawes' development through the 1630s in a comprehensible framework. An order laid out here in very tentative terms for most of the major *oeuvres* is not suggested as definitive, since all the links between style and date are still tenuous; but it seems best to take the plunge and give rough, even overlapping datings along the following lines:

1628–30:	early four-part aires
1630–4:	'old' Royall Consort (*d–D ordres*)
1635:	early fantasy and 'playnsong' a5 in *g*
1634–6:	violin setts
1637–8:	five-part viol setts
1638:	'new' Royall Consort *d–D* aires
1639–40:	six-part viol setts, and remainder of Royall Consort in symphyseal old-new versions.

This very approximate list should be made to take some account of the lesser *oeuvres*, the 'harpe consorts' and the setts for two division bass viols. It seems, merely from their adjacent position in Lawes' own playing partbooks, that the harp pieces followed shortly in time the setts for the violins, and that the pieces for basses came a little further on again.[17] Putting it this way possibly over-simplifies the final position a little. No doubt out of a similar impulse that was leading him to extend the scope of the Royall Consort by adding fantasies and pavans, Lawes began to do the same for his harp setts, and scored a row of additional pieces for them into his second scorebook (B.3), occupying ground between the six-part viol setts and the rescored Royall Consort in its new version.[18] Rather than

[17] GB-Ob, MSS Mus. Sch. D. 238–40. 238 contains bass viol parts, 239 violin parts, and 240 another violin part followed by theorbo for the harp setts and (reversed) the bass viol for the division-viol setts.

[18] GB-Ob, Mus. Sch. B.3, pp.1–29 contains the viol setts—see Lawes ed. Pinto (1979) for list, and Dodd (1980–92). Next come the harp pieces, pp. 30–47; a sequence of four pavans (the first perhaps a pavan-alman) interrupted by one fantasy in *d* in second place; Dodd (1980–92), nos.187–91 as setts nos. 7–11 (one piece per sett). Lastly comes the Royall Consort, new version, *d–D ordres*.

being separate 'setts' in themselves (as Professor Lefkowitz numbered them), these pieces were probably intended, like the additions to the Royall Consort, as amplifications of already existent setts in G, d and D. They were then added on to the back of the previously copied harp-sequence in Lawes' own partbooks; but this addition seems to have taken place when copies had already been circulated, since the pieces are wellnigh unique to the autographs and with one exception feature nowhere else.[19]

Another reason for seeing these and the bass-viol divisions as instances of Lawes' ever more grandiose plans is the subject matter. Two of the harp pavans were based on subjects extracted from works of the older generation, whether as a mark of respect or out of some request made to Lawes, cannot be told. Harp consort no. 9 in D (piece no. 189) is entitled 'Cormacke' in the bass-viol partbook D.238, a reference to the royal Irish harpist Cormacke MacDermott who served 1605–18 and whom Lawes is unlikely to have known; indicating that the harp part (for a piece that does not survive elsewhere) was scored from an original of Cormacke's design.[20] The following piece in g is entitled 'Paven of Coprario' and is as titled, a regular ternary-form pavan; derived loosely from the 'fantasy' no. 7 by Lawes' master, for two bass viols and organ (in fact a binary dance with a marked resemblance to Dowland's 'Lachrimæ' theme; possibly another member of the class of pavan-almans).[21] The bass-division setts are made up of seven pieces (nos.101–7), divided into a group of three in g and four in C, though the penultimate piece in C seems to have been abandoned. Lawes here drew similarly on a pavan–alman pair by Alfonso Ferrabosco II (now indexed as pavan no. 2 and alman no. 1, though they seem to form a natural pair in C). The organ reduction of Ferrabosco's pieces used by Lawes as backcloth is only a Tr–B outline, filled in with simplified part-movement, to set off these callisthenics (nos.104–5). More to the point, he was now in a position

[19] No. 187 occurs in GB-Och, MS Mus. 5; see Dodd (1980–92).
[20] Holman (1987) discusses the surviving output of MacDermott; see also subsequent correspondence in the same journal from Layton Ring on the instrumentation and authorship of harp works.
[21] Coprario's original in MB IX no.101; Lawes' adaptation in Coates and Dart (1955) = MB XXI, no. 11.

to regard his own works as firmly part of the repertoire, appreciable and recognisable, even in backcloth form, by the connoisseur. The first three of the bass divisions are grounded in aires from his early sett in *g* for Tr–Tr–T–B: a pavan followed by two almans (nos.101–3). Furthermore, the seventh piece for division basses is none other than a Royall Consort dance, corant no. 33 in *D*, somewhat disguised by its transposition into *C* and relegation to the organ.

As well as serving to show the apparently secure status now reached by Lawes as a modern classic, it is possible, provisionally at least, from these few straws in the wind, to place the main body of the harp works, and then the division-bass pieces, some time in the period following Lawes' royal appointment, 1635–7. It is true that the form of the corant (no. 33) employed is apparently more primitive than that in the 'old' version (Ex. 43). This in turn was worked over before inclusion in the 'new'; but that alone is not justification for giving the bass-viol divisions an early date. It is just as probable that Lawes found the extensive treble repartee that dictates the shape of the full version a distraction from the bass dialogue he was trying to elicit from the piece, and simply cut it out peremptorily, as was his wont when wishing to show (like Lewis Carroll's Humpty Dumpty) who was master.

It appears therefore that much of these contents of the scorebook B.3 are 'toppings-up'; the completion of pre-existent *oeuvres* by some of Lawes' latest writings, which applies to the major division material as well. That is of interest since one can regard the fantasies in particular, for the harp consort, as well as the Royall Consort, as indications of the direction in which Lawes would have moved, given more time. It is a highly figurate counterpoint that is not thematically as abruptly characterised as in the viol consorts; instead it substitutes an arpeggiated motivic play, partly no doubt to respect the idiom natural to players of harp and theorbo. Lawes as before is determined to start with bold skeletal themes; but there is greater use than before of repetitive rhythmic sequence as a major device of section-building. The harp-consort fantasy, as well as being in the same key, is especially close in feeling to the loping strides of Royall Consort no. 1, fantasy in d, and suits the same sort of preludial function (Ex. 44a–b).

155

Ex. 43: Corant (33)

Royall Consort (33)

Bass Viol division sett no.2 (organ)

Ex. 44a: Fantasy (191)

One last group of chamber pieces needs to be fitted somehow into the pattern: six aires, found in the composer's scorebook (B.2), groupable by threes into two setts c–C for four viols (Tr–Tr–B–B: numbered 108–13). The first piece out of each triplet has gained the modern title 'fantasy', for no better (or worse) reason than a lack of the division into binary form that marks the remainder out as 'aires' (in fact the last of them, no. 113, is tripartite, if you consider its 'close' as a fully-fledged section in itself; the middle section is in tripla notation).

Ex. 44b: Fantasy (1)

All these pieces are distinctly 'airy', inasmuch as the exceptionally florid and episodic texture has little real fugal stiffening, and is bound by no discernible formal plan; they also seem to require the glue provided by an organ backing, which for perhaps understandable reasons Lawes did not bother to score in these or indeed any of the viol works in five to six parts, where the need can be gauged only through reference to the surviving autograph organ part.[22] They are clearly intended for viol consort—as clearly, that is, as the five-part sequence in the midst of which they are found.

Casting the mind back it will be remembered that Lawes began by scoring the two early five-part fantasies in *g* into his scorebook and then, after some gap, pursued a plan of fitting them out in sett-form by adding

---

[22] Lawes ed. Taruskin (1983), ed. Nicholson (1985), the first with score, the second providing an editorial organ part by the present writer.

two fantasies in *a*, and an aire apiece to round out each group. The significant titling 'for ye Violls' was given to the first of the fantasies in a; it also occurs as 'for the Violls a4' immediately preceding in the intervening section, where these four-part setts were copied. For some reason Lawes may have set out to master the sphere of four-part fantasy just as he intended to dominate that of five parts, and at much the same time; and then (again, for some unclear reason) began to feel that this departure was taking him beyond the bounds of what was manageable. There is something just a little diffuse about the luxuriance of the passage-work, vigorous though it is; and only two of the pieces, the 'fantasy' and first aire in C (111–12), show any clear thematic linkage, with a scalar octave incipit (first up then down). The pieces are unknown elsewhere apart from the occurrence of two of them (nos. 109–10), hastily copied as late additions to the Shirley Partbooks (see Chapter I, table). Both there show minor discrepancies from the score-version, and no. 110 is actually in a different key (the violin *d*, instead of *c*).

From such small traces the composer's intentions are hard to track; but it may well be that here we have a remnant of other lost consort 'setts' in three to four parts that Henry Lawes, for one, attested were written, when he eulogised William in the memorial *Choice Psalmes* (1648) and advertised the existence of

his greater Compositions, (too voluminous for the Presse) which I the rather now mention, lest being, as they are, disperst into private hands, they may chance be hereafter lost; for, besides his Fancies of the Three, Foure, Five and Six Parts to the Viols and Organ, he hath made above thirty severall sorts of Musick for Voices and Instruments.

Murray Lefkowitz for one stated a firm belief in the former existence of autograph 'complete editions' to rival those now kept at Oxford, and time may yet vindicate him.

It would still be good to have a firmer idea of when, in the increasingly tumultuous later '30s, the music was written and—need one say it?—performed. Such, however, was the degree of political breakdown after 1639, (when disastrous failure of the royal campaign against rebellion in Scotland resulted in the overrunning of the north of England by the Scots army and a humiliating climbdown for the king, followed by parliamentary impeachment of his chief minister Strafford, who was widely feared to be planning military subjugation of England with Irish armies), that one is hardly justified in supposing any opportunity for rational planning of composing-schedules among royal musicians by this date (or for that matter any properly managed 'concert' life). Does, therefore, the bulk of Lawes' output date from before this period of ferment, or for that matter well after it, in the royalist stronghold of Oxford during the first civil war, 1642–6? The evidence from the centre is (as ever) scanty. What recent research has succeeded in doing with the means to hand is in shedding light on the activities of the small fry, collectors and copyists, who in the later 1630s were catching at whatever new repertoire was to be had.

One in particular is highly important, for the simple and circular reason that his collection survives well-preserved and perhaps even largely complete. He is significant in two further ways that derive from his sheer ordinariness: firstly, because there is no sign that he was intimate with the composers of the top rank, though he must have been on good terms with some of their lesser colleagues, who may have provided him at first hand with their own works and at second or third hand with those of the more sought-after writers; secondly, because he is representative of a far larger array of contemporaries who must have played, collected and copied music in much the same way, but have now been consigned to oblivion by the wreckage of time. There is consequently something very fitting about his commonplace name.

John Browne's interest in the progressive music of the later 1630s was possibly not predestined, since his background was solid city-merchant puritan.[23] His father Thomas (1567–1621), a freeman of the Grocers' Company, died when John was only 12. The orphaned boy was brought up in the households of his uncle John, a member of Merchant Taylors' Company, and his friend Richard Fishbourne, in the parish of St Bartholomew's, Exchange. It was a formidable business partnership operated by Browne and Fishbourne; commemorated quaintly in an

[23] Ashbee (1977).

epicedium on Fishbourne and Browne jointly (though the latter had not yet died), 'the great London benefactor & his executor', by the poet William Browne of Tavistock (no relation).[24] The rector of the parish of St Mildred in the Poultry, Nathaniel Shute, gave Fishbourne a fulsome valediction in his commemorative sermon preached in Mercers' chapel, 10 May 1625, and published as *Corona Charitatis* (1626). Dedicated to the elder John Browne, it addressed him as one, like his deceased friend, who 'loue not the common varnish of the world, and ... turne in the fairest part of your abilities from the ordinarie view'. Fishbourne had early in life come to court from his native Huntingdon as a servant to the nobility, but 'did not long like the candied hapinesse of the Court', and gravitated to the city in the employ of Sir Baptist Hickes (later created Viscount Campden, in 1628). His partner Browne did not long survive him, dying in 1627. Browne the elder's nuncupative will of 28 April 1629 (so dated, because the occasion of John Browne the younger's majority caused a posthumous family row) left £14,000 to the younger John out of his 'love and extraordinary affection'; though it is only just to note that an even larger sum, £16,000, was left to the remainder of kin and to pious uses. The younger John when scarcely out of his minority was thus a wealthy man of leisure with few immediate family ties; and though he pursued legal studies at the Middle Temple from the Michaelmas term of 1628, seems not to have practised.

From 1629 Browne engaged in land purchases in the south-west corner of Northamptonshire at Eydon, Radstone near Steane, and elsewhere in these last uplands of the Cotswolds. He held Twickenham manor house on leasehold from the queen's agents by 1636 at the latest. His first wife Temperance Crewe (daughter to Sir Thomas, and niece of Sir Randolph, two former Speakers of the House of Commons) died young on 22nd September 1634. In 1636 he married Elizabeth, the daughter of the civil servant John Packer who had been secretary to the assassinated Duke of Buckingham, George Villiers, and was still a man of standing as a clerk of the privy seal. Given that background, when a vacancy occurred for the post of Clerk

---

[24] GB-Lbl, Add. MS 30982, ff. 124–23 rev. The poet Thomas Middleton had dedicated his homiletic work *The Mariage of the Old and New Testament* (1620) to Fishbourne and Browne jointly.

of the Parliaments (which carried an overall reponsibility for upkeep of records in both Houses, and maintenance of daily business in the Lords), the unexpected appointment of Browne in March 1637/8 could have resulted from natural influences through either or both layers of his marital connections.[25]

The power exertable by trusted functionaries, such as Packer was, could be spectacular: John Boyle described in a letter (to his brother the Earl of Cork) how he had used Thomas Packer as a means of access to his brother John, in soliciting the bishopric of Cork. John Packer in turn took him to Buckingham, who brought him before King James; and 'all this in one and the same evening'.[26] In the game of patronage and mutual back-scratching, sectarian affiliations counted for surprisingly little, ability (and pliability) for all. Buckingham himself had been an ambiguous figure in the politico-religious quadrilles played out in the mid-1620s, and had been for a while tempted by puritanical doctrines—he had secured the knighthood and Speakership for the waspishly puritan Sir Thomas Crewe in 1624. Which should suffice as background to the cultural ambivalences that explain the attachment of a young well-to-do puritan to both courtly fantasy music and the newer dance of the 1630s.

As observed in Chapter II, Browne was busy acquiring dance-repertoire very soon after he came of age, supplementing the older and more traditional music that his family background had bequeathed him (this last has been assessed by Andrew Ashbee, and needs only the briefest mention here).[27] His four chief MS sets of consort books and of dances, by accident or design, are now in the library of Christ Church, Oxford, and form an important part of that important collection's holdings of instrumental music from the early Stuart period. One consort set of the fantasy repertoire in three to six parts (Mus. 423–8) seems to be from the immediate Browne family, and is our major source for the instrumental music of John Milton

[25] See *Knyvett Letters* ed. Schofield (1949), 92 for the disappointment of another suitor for the post.
[26] Quoted from the Lissmore Papers by Morgan (1957), 76; see further in this study for a useful general discussion of the influence of John Preston on the circle of Packer and Crewe.
[27] Ashbee (1977).

the elder, scrivener of Bread Street and father of the great poet, including an unusual In Nomine a6 with a texted tenor cantus firmus line to pious words. Another, Mus. 473–8, could have reached Browne from in-laws of either marriage, though more probably from the Crewe side.

The significance behind his commissioning of hand-copied sets, that give a broad picture of the dance-music in three to four parts of the early '30s is hard to overstate, since without it the important stage (discussed in Chapter II) in the evolution of dance towards Lawes' Royall Consort, which Browne is not known to have possessed, would be almost invisible. It may serve too, if any further evidence is yet needed, to bolster the rebuttal given long since by Percy Scholes to the notion of puritans as an anti-musical dance-hating faction in society. One has only to recall the career of the lawyer Bulstrode Whitelocke, who procured Lawes and Simon Ives to write the score for the *Triumph of Peace* in 1633–4, to scotch that unthinking assumption.[28] We cannot, though, tell how catholic the tastes of Browne were in comparison to the lost collections of his contemporaries; nor, lacking that gauge, whether he acquired new music as soon as composers allowed it to enter circulation, or whether he was a year or two behind the style-leaders in his acquisitions. One suspects that as a genuine enthusiast he was in the forefront; acquiring the violin setts of Lawes by the period 1636–8, for example, when they cannot have been long in the hands of professional copyists.[29] As a very probable early user, therefore, Browne's copies of Lawes' consort setts for viols throw light, in several almost incidental ways, on the way they were brought into general circulation, and at another level on their likely time of composition and assemblage.

The extent to which Browne was bowled over by hearing—the operative term, perhaps—the viol consorts of William Lawes is shown in a singular act of homage. At the end of the five-part section in his partbook set Mus. 473–8, Browne added four pieces that together make up a consort sett along the lines developed by Lawes. It is composed of an 'Ayre' (alman), an 'In nomine fantazia', next an untitled

[28] See Scholes (1934); Ashbee (1982).
[29] Lawes ed. Pinto (1991) discusses the range of possible dates for Browne's copies of these violin works.

Ex. 45a: In nomine fantazia J[ohn] B[rowne]

6

Ex. 45b: Fantasy (94)

Ex. 45c: Pavin   J[ohn] B[rowne]

alman and lastly a 'Pavin', all in five parts and all in the unusual key (for large-scale viol consort, that is) of *B* flat. This sett is headed self-effacingly 'J.B.', though the authorship would have been plain to acquaintances, from the unmistakable italic hand of the owner-copyist. The most arresting feature is that Browne followed Lawes in transposing the plainsong for the In Nomine into the major mode, an otherwise unprecedented step in the whole history of the form; no-one else, however iconoclastic, rethought the process to this extent. Browne's pavan goes on to quote the opening of Lawes' fantasy.

Another point of note is that Browne scored his sett for a five-part consort that made use of the standard two-treble dialogue; but instead of scoring the lower voices for T–T–B, he chose the at first sight unusual T–B–B combination, one used from time to time in the five-part Jacobean repertoire, but never favoured as a norm.[30] Is this a sign that, before going out to find or commission copies of Lawes' consort setts, Browne had relied on the evidence of eye and ear, and decided to write his own pieces in a scoring that he had just seen performed? (Ex. 45a–c). There is a procedural ambiguity inherent in any stave music, which in itself does no more than hint at correct instrumentation, unless of course extra-musical directions are included. Browne could well have seen a professional realisation upon a Tr–Tr–T–2B ensemble, even if the clefs to us imply a two-tenor scoring. In fact the clefs employed by Lawes for line IV in his five-part setts underwent alteration at a key point, just when he decided to forge ahead with a sett-plan for fantasies. The first two fantasies in *g* were scored for Tr–Tr–T–T–B in the regular clefs, G2–C3–F4. When Lawes came to add the fantasies in *a* and the two aires in *g* and *a* accompanying them, he changed the clef of the fourth line to C4, which could imply use of a larger instrument—either a large tenor,

---

[30] Two out of above 50 fantasies by Coprario have this scoring; the proportion is 2/32 in the case of Lupo. Ward and Jenkins seem not to acknowledge the possibility. Only the first two pieces by Browne show the 2B scoring, simply because the others exist just in the Cantus part (Mus. 473).

Ex. 46a: Ayre (1)   J[ohn] B[rowne]

still strung in tenor tuning, or a small bass. The remainder of the five-part setts stick to the use of clef C4 on line IV. It seems then that Browne had witnessed performances of both five- and six-part setts by Lawes before writing his own imitations. His decision to include a pavan in his own sett suggests that the *B* flat pieces by Lawes were not the only extract he had heard, since the *B* flat sett contains no pavan. Only one other piece in the six-part sequence by Lawes is in pavan form, compared to three of those in the five-part sequence. The first 'Ayre' makes an intriguing comparison with the aire in *B* flat by Lawes (no. 95). Browne shows signs of having absorbed the two-treble interplay found in bars 15–20 of Lawes' aire in his last few bars (semibreve pulse, bars 38–42; see Ex. 46a–b).

It would be pleasant to be able to announce the discovery of musical value in these pieces by Browne, but apart from their general utility in pointing up features of their models it is hard to discover any. In writing them he left some clues to tempo-variation as well as instrumentation: his markings suggest that variation was expected

166

Ex. 46b: Air (95)

in dances (both pavan and alman) as well as fantasies. In his first alman the second strain bears the direction 'drag' (implying either rallentando, or direct transition to a slower tempo) in the top three voices at its beginning, and the contrary direction 'come of[f]' (to suggest transition to faster tempo) after a pause bar, 35. It suggests that players had considerable liberty by this time to 'humour' the pieces, by applying a rubato that Thomas Mace would have commended, forty years on. The second alman contains the direction 'come of', following the median double bar, followed by a 'drag', and even a three-bar-long tripla; the 'Pavin' also conforms to the pattern of faster–slower in both second and third strains. Even in the In Nomine work where an unvarying tempo could easily be assumed from the assumption of regular tactus, there are frequent indications of variation: a 'drag' within the confines of one breve's (bar's) space is followed immediately and quite abruptly by 'come of'(Ex. 47).

These pieces also offer another angle to approach the so far timid answer to the question about time of composition for Lawes' models. Because the last two pieces in Browne's sett were copied only in

Ex. 47: In nomine fantazia   J[ohn] B[rowne]

the Cantus partbook (Mus. 473), it seems that something came in the way of completing the copies. Sheer caprice, perhaps? Or external circumstances? There are in fact other pieces in Browne's partbook sets apparently by him which show the same signs of interruption. Mus. 379–81, his three-part collection, has in last position an unattributed Tr–Tr–B sett in *c*, consisting of a pavan–alman–corant sequence.[31] The bass part was copied into partbook 381, but he found opportunity to write down little more than six bars of the pavan's beginning into the treble book. It seems unlikely that boredom overcame him in the composing of setts of works simultaneously, and in looking for an event that upset his copying programme one is tempted to look at the whole concatenation of events around 1642 that led to

[31] GB-Och, 379–81 source nos. 67–9: 'Pauan a.3. 2 Trebles', 'Almaine a.3 2 Trebbles', [untitled].

civil war; not least because some exterior force seems to have separated Browne from his musical collection.

It is clear that after the end of major hostilities in 1649 Browne like many others parted company with the emergent Commonwealth regime, and pursued his life as a Northampton country squire until the Restoration offered him a chance of rejoining the capital's polite society. (He found it wise at this point to sign his assent to the terms of the Declaration of Breda, guaranteeing amnesty for most classes of the former king's enemies, but seems to have found no difficulty in resuming his career.) Northamptonshire had for some time been the focus of his life: both his daughters married local boys, as Sydney Tyrell's study of village life in Eydon remarks.[32] Music was apparently respected in the family of his son-in-law Sir Roger Cave, since additions to the musical part of the library were made in the later 17th century, and some part of Browne's own outmoded fantasy music was preserved assiduously in the family until sold earlier in the 20th century.[33] How, then, to explain the appearance of some of the more valuable of Browne's musical possessions in the college of Christ Church by the later 17th century, in the musical collection of the college's Dean, Henry Aldrich?

The cause that cut Browne off from these very personal treasures will not have been a trivial one; and one is forced to consider the possibility that he lost them inadvertently through some sort of seizure in wartime. If so, it reduces the time-scale considerably for Browne to have heard, imitated and acquired Lawes' consort setts. The cumulative internal evidence has been stated above for seeing the completion of the six-part setts (including that in B flat, imitated by Browne) as around the year 1640 at the earliest. Since hostilities broke out in later 1642 and the king set up court that autumn in Oxford, it does not seem conceivable that Browne could have been venturing beyond London after that time.

[32] Tyrell (1973), 25–33, 58–9, 272–4.
[33] Pinto (1978). Sets now in the Rowe Library of King's College, Cambridge, are among the pieces to have resurfaced this century; see Ashbee (1977). The division of items made in the 17th century did not respect the integrity of sets: for example, an organ part to Browne's copy of Lawes' violin setts has been at Christ Church for nigh on three centuries, now listed as MS Mus. 430; one separate violin part, combining copies of Lawes' and Coprario's similar setts, has emerged into private hands from sales by present representatives of his family within the last half-century.

169

Like many of the law officers with fixed abode, he stayed in London (it was only circuit judges who were mobile enough to flock to Oxford, for example), and earned himself considerable disapprobation from the royalists, if only for the reason that his name appeared on the title-page of all acts and ordinances of the wartime parliament, which was compelled to legislate without the sanction of the king's seal.[34] Communicating with his younger brothers-in-law, with whom he seems to have played Lawes' violin works (to judge from an inscription within his organ part, now Christ Church MS Mus 430) would have been out of the question, whether they stayed at home in Berkshire or came to their Oxford college for company. At the time of course no-one could have guessed how severe hostilities were to become, or how long they were to last.

In a way the story of Lawes' viol consorts ends with a whimper, and no great bang. There is little trace remaining of his wartime activities, or even evidence that he was much at Oxford, though one is more or less forced to assume it for lack of any other locality. Nor is there any real clues to brother Henry's whereabouts, though it could be that he spent the war in London, observing hostilities from what to a monarch's servant were the sidelines, if not the opponent's goalmouth. An odd little setting was tucked onto an already copied page in his autograph songbook, which later figured in expanded form in the *Choice Psalmes* of 1648, and seems to show his feelings at this isolation, based on George Sandys' paraphrase of Psalm 120, 5–7: 'woe is mee, y[t] I from Israell exiled, must in Mesech dwell & in the Tents of Ismael.'.[35] Since the three-part psalms that Henry published from William's pen are so apt for the campaigning chapel (when the royal singing-men would have been in short supply) it would be pleasant in a way to believe that Henry together with his brother had been on hand to solace the king's religious devotions; but despite the

---

[34] Pinto (1978).
[35] GB-Lbl, Add. MS 53723 f. 18, for single voice (clef C1) and unfigured basso line. The same music reappeared set à3 in the section of *Choice Psalmes* devoted to Henry's works, no. xi. The hand that copied this short piece is very much more mature than the foliation would suggest, and it is clearly the germ of a passing idea almost casually jotted. The same is true of a setting 'Thy beauty Israell is fled', added to a similar interstice on f. 54; also to a text by Sandys, but with much slighter resemblance to the version worked up in *Choice Psalmes*. See Willetts (1969) for contents.

dedication of the published version of 1648 insisting that the works were 'born and nourish'd' in the king's service, there is no exterior evidence to link them to wartime usage.

A striking portrait of a musician in his forties was painted by William Dobson at Oxford in mid-1645, which has some claim to consideration as William Lawes pictured in the final summer of his life, amid the last rays of hope that were to gild the royalist cause for many a year. There is of course no definite proof that this subject was Lawes. One expert has found a striking similarity in treatment of the brow region to the attested portrait of Henry Lawes, presented by him to the Oxford Music School's collection. (The differences are great enough to show that the Dobson portrait cannot be Henry.) An assumed genuine portrait of Lawes also kept in the Oxford Music School collection has some intriguing similarities to, and also differences from, Dobson's work, possibly to be explained by a naive approach to the planes of the face in the earlier likeness that gives it such sharp mercurial features, and show up the later face as comparatively commonplace and puffy (and yet more naturalistic). If it were a question of choosing one or the other piece, it should be borne in mind that the Oxford portrait of a younger man was presented in the 18th century by the Professor of Music, Philip Hayes, and has no impeccable pedigree to offer if authenticity is the watchword. From 1643 Dobson had become more or less official limner to the Oxford court for the duration, and in 1645 one of his numerous commissions was of Charles Gerard (later 1st Earl of Macclesfield), Lawes' commanding officer, according to the early account by Thomas Fuller.[36] Whatever Lawes' commission, and however roving it was, he also, like Gerard, could have been back and forth from Oxford at this time, before the fatal shortages of personnel and *matériel* that increasingly afflicted the king's forces during the year were felt to the full and (possibly) resulted in the secondment of Lawes as commissary, to drum up supplies.

There is musical evidence—for what that is worth—that Lawes may have participated in some capacity in the Siege of York, 22 April to

---

[36] For both Gerrard and the unknown musician see Rogers (1983), nos. 38, 41. The latter is reproduced in Lawes ed. Pinto (1991) = *MB* LX. Fuller's account, from his *Worthies of England* (1662), is given by Lefkowitz (1960).

14th July 1644. Some remarkable psalm-settings by him survive in the library of Christ Church, copied by Edward Lowe (and unique to it, apart from a partial score of one of the psalms, 22, in a contemporary Durham Cathedral MS).[37] They combine verses written in a florid style for very capable solo voices, over a basso continuo line, with choruses not in traditional choral style but in the form of the very downmarket hymn-tunes that the Protestant laity had taken to its bosom and refused to relinquish at any price. The combination is unique, and can only denote a tactful compromise between liturgically opposed forces, between a puritan-inclined congregation and a high-church, sophisticated body of cathedral singers. It so happens that the only recorded occasion on which such a combination was tried out was in York Minster, during the siege of the royalist garrison by a joint Anglo-Scottish force, as noted by Murray Lefkowitz. The coincidence is a little too great to be passed off, especially as there is other evidence, from one of Lawes' rounds made off-the-cuff, that he was in the neighbourhood of York by May 1644.[38] It would be entirely appropriate if the last recorded compositions by Lawes were intended to repair rents in the fabric of the times, by the expedient of juxtaposing the same centrifugal forces of which his own chamber writings show an acute awareness.

There are no signs that general acquaintance with his consort music so much as survived the civil wars, apart from the existence of a couple of later copies for which no firm date is yet possible, that indicate some limited circulation in degraded versions of varying corruptness. Christ Church library still has a set of the six-part pieces, combined with copies of the Royall Consort, new version; they are dependent in some unknown way upon the copies owned by John Browne, which they resemble uncannily.[39] The British Library holds

[37] GB-Och, MSS Mus. 768–70; GB-DRc, MS B.1, pp. 97–107.
[38] Lefkowitz (1960), 249–56; Pinto (1986), 579–583. The only published examples of these pieces are of 'The Lamentation' and Psalm 47 ed. Dodd (1970) = Church Choir Library, no. 675.
[39] GB-Och, MSS Mus. 479–83. There may well be undiscovered links between the two major pre-Commonwealth musical libraries. Browne and Hatton, both Northamptonshire men, that have found a home at Christ Church. Both came into the possession of Henry Aldrich (d. 1710) and after that to the college by bequest. Whether Hatton acquired (say) the music of Browne as spoils of war would be impossible to say at the moment.

another late set of parts, known to and used by Arnold Dolmetsch, but unfortunately given to bursting into strings of gibberish from time to time. The set apparently had an organ part now lost, which one would have liked to see if only to satisfy curiosity about how it coped with the points where the partbooks fall out between themselves.[40] It makes one consider seriously the point raised by Francis Baines, that for a time patrons may have wanted the prestige of owning a copy of these works, unplayed, and for little more purpose than to adorn their bookshelves, in the way that many nowadays would possess (say) *Finnegan's Wake* as a conversation piece rather than for personal pleasure. But styles in music-making were changing, and with the exception of collectors who were strong-minded enough to swim against the tide, like Christopher Baron Hatton, the days of the ensemble in five to six parts were numbered.

In another late survival, Lawes' five-part consort setts are found in a partbook once actually owned by Dr Burney, and now at Yale University. However the more significant part of the music consists of overtures, sonatas etc. by Henry Purcell (some part in his own hand) and his younger contemporaries; though it has a unique part for a 'Newark set' in 4 parts by Jenkins, and other lyra consorts by him, elsewhere unrecorded. Only the bass part survives today; as pointed out by Robert Ford, it is a 'guard-book', into which were sewn and glued a miscellany of different copies, each on their own paper.[41] That containing the five-part works of Lawes could therefore have been (probably was) copied considerably earlier than the remainder, and simply included for its potential as exercise for the trio-sonata generation.[42] Notably, when still in Burney's library, three

---

[40] GB-Lbl, Add. MSS 29410–5. See Lawes ed. Pinto (1979).
[41] Yale University, Beinecke Library, Osborn Collection, MS 515; see Ford (1983).
[42] Lawes ed. Pinto (1979) dates the MS as of the 1660s, a typing error which should have been 1690s; though even that would need revaluation, if all the individual fascicles were to be assessed separately. See *The Late Dr. Burney's Musical Library* (Mon. 8 Aug. 1814) as sold by White: GB-Lbl, S.C.1076.(1.); 5th Day, Lot 633, acquired by Picart; and the sale of the Rev. Samuel Picart's collection (10 Mar. 1848) by Puttick and Simpson, Lot 208, when three partbooks were still extant. This is probably the MS sold in Gostling's sale of 1777, 2nd Day, Lot 13: see King (1963) for a general guide to sales.

partbooks were extant; though he would not have had the chance to form a worthwhile judgement from that remnant. It is quite likely that the three parts (Tr–Tr–B) had been selected from an older complete set, by whoever made up these partbooks, just as a residue that might yet be worth consideration for an up-to-date ensemble in the 1680s or later. In support of this, it is observable that the one piece out of Lawes' five-part setts which would work least well in the trio-sonata combination, the 'Playnsong' in *g*, has been omitted from the copy.

The story of Lawes' death in battle can only be unravelled by a campaign expert. It appears that Lawes was in Chester as part of the diminished royal force, in the dismal autumn of 1645 as the king was losing more and more of his foothold in the main territory of England, and forced to fall back on Wales where loyal feeling was still high. The action around Chester was a messy one, even by usual military standards. The garrison of the city felt emboldened to make a sortie by horse, in order to rescue detached forces in a pincer movement which went horribly wrong when the biter was bit. Royalist soldiers were mown down under fire, or pursued many a weary mile, through a long day's carnage, into the territory south of the city, as far as Beeston Castle which was holding out for the king. Where and how exactly Lawes met his end in this series of skirmishes is unclear. Some were fortunate enough to escape relatively unscathed. Among them were the troops of Sir Herbert Price, who had taken part in the defence of Chester, and were at the battle on Rowton Heath on the 24th of September. Both Henry and Thomas Vaughan, the self-styled 'Silurists', appear to have been in this force. Henry Vaughan, the poetic 'Swan of Usk', recorded the loan of a cloak in his verse to Mr J. Ridsley thanking him for the assistance, in an action where many seem to have been forced to swim the waters of 'the fatal Dee' to escape extermination.

As for Lawes, his bones were in principle honoured. King Charles, obviously appalled by an action that left dead a close kinsmen of his own, Bernard Stuart, is reported to have had the grace to put on special mourning for Lawes, according to the account given by Thomas Fuller.[43] It is unlikely that Lawes received separate burial; the very minor poet Thomas Jordan wrote an inscription for his urn, but this may owe most to poetic licence.[44] The original of this verse has played tag with the world so long that it is worth giving it in its printed form, though it has become well-known in a manuscript form, written into a musical (keyboard) partbook:

> *An Epitaph on Mr. Will.* Lawes *Batcheler in Musick,*
> *who was mortally shot at the siege of* Westchester.
>
> *Concord is conquer'd: In this Urne there lies*
> *The Master of great Musick's mysteries,*
> *And in it is a riddle like the* cause:
> Will. Lawes *was slain by such whose* wills *were* laws.

Thus, within a short while, the insistence on 'concord', an emphasis due to the small political capital that could be gleaned from the stubble where the sword had passed, was obscuring the real adventurousness of the music. Lawes was no Orpheus torn apart by the antimusical wolves of misrule, as Robert Heath, another overenthusiastic elegist, would have had it. The trope was echoed by John Tatham in a flippant would-be witty verse 'On the Report of Master William Lawes his Death': 'He that to *Discord* could pure *Concord* give, instructing all *Society* to live'.[45] If (to be charitable) this means

---

[43] Lefkowitz (1960), 20 *ff*. Robert Herrick seems to have been close to campaign affairs, to the extent of honouring Lord Bernard Stuart in exceedingly similar terms to those employed for Lawes in the anonymous elegy set by John Jenkins: *Hesperides* (1647–8), no. ccxix, 'Hence, hence, profane'.

[44] Jordan (n.d.), sig. [A]8v. An almost identical version of this was added to the front of GB-Lbl, Add. MS 29290, f. iv, in an early 19th-century hand which may be that of the Gresham Professor Edward Taylor, a former owner of this keyboard source. Prefatory verses by Jordan to Playford (1673) contain another version of these lines in the course of his commendation of Playford: 'When by the Fury of the *Good Old Cause* / *Will. Lawes* was slain, by such whose *Wills* were *Laws*' See Lefkowitz (1960), 37.

[45] Heath (1650), Elegies pp. 9–10, 'On the Death of that most famous Musician M^r W Lawes', ll. 7–8: 'By Wolves our *Orpheus* thus oppos'd was slain; / His Lyres offended strings thus crackt in twain'. T[atham] (1650), 111–12.

anything, it could be a lame recognition that underneath the rugged surface tangles of the music lay appealingly direct and uncomplicated harmonic structures; but one suspects, from the speed with which the most recondite of his chamber works passed out of currency (insofar as one can tell), that this lip-service did not extend to active enthusiasm for chamber music.

In contrast, the Royall Consort was to an extent a beneficiary of the 'troubles'; it offered exactly the sort of cheering recreation that the war-weary could assimilate, an emblem of an ideal social order that for a time must have seemed irrecoverable. Copies obviously proliferated for a while, even after the Restoration in 1660. The whole opus, though, may not have survived for long in the full-dress scoring of the new version that the composer had spent so much effort in perfecting, since it is noticeable how the two great fantasies in d–D, and some of the pavans (especially no. 49, in C, but also no. 8 in d and 42 in a) drop out of, or are strangely defective in, the latest copies. It seems that some of them (to hazard a guess from incompletely extant sets) were soon slimmed-down to a more basic Tr–Tr–B version, packing into which the intricacies of the real six-part pieces made no sense. Some versions tried apparently to combine more than one scoring; like the set of books (now incomplete) written as late as 1680 by the Turkey merchant Sir Gabriel Roberts, and containing a good text for almost the whole of the Royall Consort: apparently first copied in a three-part form, and then with the now missing tenor part tracked down to complete it.[46] However men of wide taste, in sympathy with the past like Sir Gabriel, were exceptions.

The extent to which Lawes' abrupt and innovative linear style in dance influenced the succeeding generation or two is so far uncharted ground, and beyond present aims. Though one can be convinced that

[46] For Roberts see Thompson (1988), 367–86; Charteris (1993), and his following letter on provenance, M&L lxxv (1994), 659. In the recently rediscovered partbooks, Roberts seems to have acquired, or even had reworked, some pieces in 2Tr–2B by Lawes that had not begun in that form; so that the scoring cannot be said to have died out rapidly. See Charteris (1993), though in the absence of a complete set of partbooks for the pieces it is impossible to be sure how they were scored. The partbooks belonging to Edward Lowe as discussed above, GB-Ob, Mus. Sch. MSS D.233–6, E.451, also made an attempt to combine two versions and also are no longer complete.

the English dissonance of Christopher Gibbons and Matthew Locke, colleagues born in the 1620s, would have been more subdued without the example of Lawes behind them, the path by which the later-century orchestral style developed between 1640 and the Restoration awaits investigation. There is reason to presume that the 'string-quartet' scoring was already employed in the theatres before the civil war, from its occurrence in a set of books credibly linked to Lawes' friend Simon Ives, a London wait. It was Ives who set Bulstrode Whitelocke's coranto, transforming what one can imagine to have been a meagre sketch for a piece into a full-scale version for Tr–Tr–T–B–bc that survives in these books; but that this is identical to the version that Whitelocke remembered in self-congratulatory fashion to have been called for in the Blackfriars playhouse is an assumption for which there is no direct evidence.[47] The picture so far to be drawn is of Lawes surviving, after no more than a few years following his death, only as a diffuse influence; as an arresting gesture now and again, or as a facial expression that can be fleetingly glimpsed in relatives who never encountered the living features but relive them willy-nilly. There are worse memorials one could have.

One expectation, that is not on available evidence realised, is of any specific acknowledged borrowing (or even unacknowledged debt) in the chamber music of that paragon of composers Henry Purcell, born and dead almost exactly fifty years behind Lawes. There is nothing very remarkable in this, given that the whole of Purcell's education was spent in reaching out to sundered traditions in church and instrumental music and establishing a continuity of the sort that Lawes was striving away from. Counterpoint in its most gisty form was a perpetual delight to Purcell; Lawes has been called 'hypercontrapuntal', which is true enough if one takes it to mean a playful abnegation of the constraints that strict imitation imposes.

There is no sign that Purcell ever copied or looked at a chamber work of Lawes, which makes the well-known comments in his *Sonnata's* of 1683 the more pointed. The really rather priggish manifesto of its preface, recommending that the English 'should begin to loath the levity, and balladry of our neighbours' has been widely and doubtless correctly construed as a rebuff to French fashions; and

---

[47] GB-Lbl, Add. MSS 18940–4; see Holman (1993).

Purcell does explicitly request a turning back to the pure fount of Italy for models. His parade of apparently anti-French animus has always seemed a little strange, given that in his orchestral music he has no qualms about assimilating what he wants from that source. It should not be forgotten though that French influence goes back a long way, even before the accession of Charles I and his French consort, in whose reign it reached its apogee. Purcell was by implication repudiating a long-standing Anglo-Gallic evolved style which might with equal justice have been thought of as grown native. It goes a stage further than the chauvinist claim of Matthew Locke, in the preface to his three-part opus *The Little Consort* (1651; published 1656), made in order to answer 'those *Mountebanks of wit*, who think it necessary to disparage all they meet with of their owne Countrey-mens, because there have been and are some excellant things done by Strangers'; that he 'never yet saw any *Forain I[n]strumental Composition* (a few *French Corants* excepted) worthy an *English* mans Transcribing'.

Just as surely as Burney was to do, Purcell probably was turning his back upon the naive tunefulness of a whole epoch, whose recreational or dance music was still very much in circulation into Purcell's boyhood, but which must have begun to rankle with him for its lack of engagement. A very different type of baroque counterpoint was about to be born that redefined the acceptable limits of melodiousness, and past methods had to be swept away. In that process something unique and capable in its own ways of reaching greatness was put to one side and never again re-examined. There is an incorrigible core of lightness to Lawes even at his most serious, a grace even in the most savagely twisted lines. The vitality that so carelessly could fill large-scale forms out of the most episodic detail, by his remarkably exact ear for sonorities and motivic development, was combined with an intelligence that increasingly came to terms with valued traditions which fast-changing times were in danger of leaving behind. Obviously this would have matured if he had lived longer, since he had already shown himself so capable of creating his own standards.

All of which puts him on a very unusual plane. Without special pleading it is hard to know how to insist that chamber music of a long-dead era is just as vital as more recent contributions, and it somehow

178

seems a misdirection of energies to fight that issue. One recalls the occasion when Rupert Erlebach addressed the Musical Association on the topic of Lawes' largely unmined seam of chamber music, only to be held up to his phraseology after speaking by one Dr. Froggart:

I understand the lecturer to make some comparison between the string music of Lawes and the last five quartets of Beethoven; I cannot follow him there. These works of Lawes are among the early flowers of modern instrumental music; but the last five quartets of Beethoven come from another world.

Mr Erlebach:

That was a quotation from *The Musical Standard* ... It is not my opinion.'

This is a little mealy-mouthed, even as a defence made on the hop against an unexpected flank attack. A generation or two on, when, for example, the scales that weigh Beethoven against Mozart have once more trembled in the other direction, it seems futile to indulge in spats like this on such unequal territory; though a time may come when two very different type of chamber music can be amicably compared. Lawes however no longer needs profuse apology. He has his own internal and cohesive development that fits a pattern to which all talents recognised as great conform, even if they are not given time enough to do more than offer a hint of what they could have achieved under more favourable circumstances. With very little trouble he can be assessed fairly for importance in the terms of his own age, which are not beyond our wit to reconstruct.

The problems are twofold: firstly that, very much like Monteverdi, Lawes employed eclectic methods in a time when theoretical justifications were probably impossible to formulate. (Monteverdi never succeeded in setting pen to paper in the task that his brother heralded for him.) A decision to abandon strict counterpoint in favour of other methods (even less specified than Monteverdi's) cut no ice in the formative period of music history-writing. Secondly, again like Monteverdi (who died just two years before Lawes), Lawes was born into a period of discontinuity, so that only a refracted version of his achievements was passed on. It no longer seems a problem with Monteverdi and, given time and greater exposure to the sounds of the music, should not stand in the way of a fairer estimation of Lawes. His major work, nonetheless, by being predominantly instrumental, rises to a class of chamber music that makes large claims for itself: by its scale, and by the types of musical experiences that it supplants, both sacred and secular. In that degree, it prefigures the hope of a complete and wholly personal absolute language more familiar from late classical and romantic chamber music. The problem then lies in the extent to which one can take any and every aspect of his age seriously.

The brief assessment offered here of the way in which his work matures would do him no justice by divorcing it from the troubled times in which he lived. Within four years of his death the Whitehall chamber organ and viols were sold for a song, part of the general sale of royal property to defray the large costs of civil war. There was nothing on quite the same level of significance to follow the lead of Lawes in extending the concept of a suite-form, one embracing both old-fashioned fantasy and new-fangled dance-movements on which he pinned his colours; and variegated colours they were, in an assortment of inventive chamber scorings that were not equalled for over a century. The heroism and the dashed hopes implicit in his project are most fittingly bade farewell in a contemporary, half-satirical lament, nine months after the flight of the court from London in 1642, *A Deep Sigh Breathd Through the Lodgings at White-Hall*:

> At the Lodgings of the severall Lords and Gentlemen, where the smell and odour of the perfumes and tinctures of a mornings curling, and dressing, made your attendance not seem tedious but gave a delight to your frequent and long solicitation, now there's nothing but the raw sent of moist walls, and all as silent as midnight. ...
>
> If at any time you desire to see any body in, or neere the Court, that belongs to it, goe just about the shutting in of evening, And then perhaps, you may see one creeping away with a Sack of Coles on his back, another with a bundle of Fagots, another with bottells of Wine, another bartering with a Vineger man about certain Vessells of decaied beare, &c. for every thing would live by i'ts owne element as long as it can: But when all's gone, they'l be all gone too, and will be within a very short time If the times doe not alter.

Thus you see poore White-Hall is miserably deserted of all its darlings, from Majesty to muckery, forsaken and left in the most solitary condition that ever any Princes Court of so great eminence and Hospitality in the whole World was.

In the Cockpit and Revelling Roomes, where at a Play or Masque the darkest night was converted to the brightest Day that ever shin'd, by the luster of Torches, the sparkling of rich Jewells, and the variety of those incomparable and excellent Faces, from whence the other derived their brightnesse, where beauty sat inthron'd in so full a glory, that had not Phaeton fir'd the World, there had not wanted a Comparative whereunto to paralell the refulgence of their bright-shining splendor, Now you may goe in without a Ticket or the danger of a broken-pate, you may enter at the Kings side, walke round about the Theaters, view the Pullies, the Engines, conveyances, or contrivances of every several Scaene And not an Usher o'th Revells, or Engineere to envy or finde fault with your discovery, although they receive no gratuitie for the sight of them.

Bibliography

Place of publication is London unless otherwise stated.

Abbey, Hermione, 'Sir Peter Leycester's Book on Music', *JVdGSA* xxi (1984) 28–44
[Arkwright, G. E. P.], 'A Paven by William Lawes', *MA* i (1909–10), 108–18
Arnold, Cecily and Johnson, Marshall, 'The English Fantasy Suite', *PRMA* lxxxii (1955–6), 1–14
Ashbee, Andrew, 'Instrumental Music from the Library of John Browne (1608–1691), Clerk of the Parliaments', *M&L* lviii (1977), 43–59
—'A Not Unapt Scholar: Bulstrode Whitelocke (1605–1675),' *Chelys* , xi (1982), 24–31
—*Records of English Court Music* (Snodland, 1986–91, Aldershot, 1991–)
—*The Harmonious Musick of John Jenkins* I (Surbiton, 1992)
Aubrey, John, *Aubrey on Education* ed. J. E. Stephens (1972)
Aylmer, G.E., *The King's Servants* (1961; 2/1974)
—*The State's Servants* (1973)
Banister, John and Low, Thomas (eds.) *New Aires and Dialogues* (1678)
Bentley, Gerald Eades, *The Jacobean and Caroline Stage, VI: Theatres* (Oxford, 1968)
Bianconi, Lorenzo, *Music in the The Seventeenth Century* (Cambridge, 1987)
Brown, Cedric C., *John Milton's Aristocratic Entertainments* (Cambridge, 1985)
Buch, David Joseph, 'The Influence of the *Ballet de cour* in the Genesis of the French Baroque Suite', *AM* lvii (1985), 94–109
Burney, Charles, *A General History of Music* (1776–89; R/ed. Frank Mercer, 1935; 2/ New York, 1957)
—*The Letters of Dr Charles Burney I: 1751–1784* ed. Alvaro Ribeiro (Oxford, 1991)
Burwell Lute Tutor, The, intr. Robert Spencer (F/Leeds, 1974)
Butler, Charles, *The principles of musik* (1636; F/ New York, 1970, intr. Gilbert Reaney)
Butler , Gregory J., 'The Fantasia as Musical Image', *MQ* lx (1974), 602–15
—'Music and Rhetoric in Early Seventeenth-Century English Sources', *MQ* lxvi (1980), 53–64
Butler, Henry, *Collected Works,* ed. Elizabeth V. Phillips (Madison, 1991) = *RRMBE* LXVI
Caldwell, John, *English Keyboard Music before the Nineteenth Century* (Oxford, 1973)
—*The Oxford History of Music , I ... to c.1715* (Oxford, 1991)
Campbell, Margaret, *Dolmetsch: The Man and his Work* (1975)
—'Not Quite Eye to Eye: Percy Scholes and Arnold Dolmetsch', *The Consort* n. s. i (1994), 95–110
Chan, Mary, *Music in the Theatre of Ben Jonson* (Oxford, 1980)
[Charles I], *The King's Cabinet Opened,* in *Harleian Miscellany* VII (1811), 559
Charteris, Richard, 'Autographs of John Coprario', *M&L* lvi (1975), 41–6
—'John Coprario's Five and Six-Part Pieces: Instrumental or Vocal?' *M&L* lvii (1976), 370–8

Charteris, Richard, *John Coprario: A Thematic Catalogue of his Music* (New York, 1977)

—'Music Manuscripts and Books Missing from Archbishop Marsh's Library, Dublin', *M&L* lxi (1980), 310–17

—'A Rediscovered Manuscript Source ... ' *Chelys*, xxii (1993), 3–29

Coates, William and Dart, Thurston (eds.), *Jacobean Consort Music* (1955; 2/1962; 3/1971) = *MB* IX

Coleman, Charles, ed. W. H. Davis (1971) = *SP* 81

Cooper, B. A. R., 'The Keyboard Suite in England before the Restoration', *M&L* liii (1972), 309–19

Coprario, John, *Giovanni Coperario: Rules how to Compose (c.1610),* intr. Manfred F. Bukofzer (Los Angeles, 1952)

—*The Five-Part Pieces,* ed. Richard Charteris (Stuttgart, 1981) = *CMM* XCII

—*The Six-Part Consorts and Madrigals,* ed. Richard Charteris (Clifden, 1982)

Craig-McFeely, Julia, 'A Can of Worms: Lord Herbert of Cherbury's Lute Book', *The Lute (= LSJ),* xxxi (1991) 20–47

Cunningham, James P., 'The Country Dance: Early References', *JEFDSS* ix (1961), 148–54

—*Dancing in the Inns of Court* (1965)

Cunningham, Walker, *The Keyboard Music of John Bull* (Ann Arbor, 1984)

Cutts, J. P., 'Robert Johnson and the Court Masque' *M&L* xli (1960), 111–26

—'Drexel MS 4041', *MD* xviii (1964), 151–201

Davies, D. W., *Elizabethans Errant* (Cornell, 1967)

Dean-Smith, Margaret and Nicol, E. J., '"The Dancing Master": 1651–1728, Part II: Country Dance and Revelry before 1651', *JEFDSS* iv (1944) 167–179; Part III: 'Our Country Dances', *JEFDSS* iv (1945), 211–31

Deep Sigh Breathd Through the Lodgings at White-Hall , A (1642); GB-Lbl, E.119 (30)

De Lauze, F., *Apologie de la Danse* (n. pl. [Paris?], 1623)

—*A Treatise of Instruction in Dancing and Deportment,* trans. and ed. Joan Wildeblood (1952)

Dent, Edward J., *Foundations of English Opera* (Cambridge, 1928; R/New York 1965)

Dering, Richard, ed. Richard Nicholson (1981) = *ECS* xii

Dictionary of National Biography: Missing Persons, The ed. C. S. Nicholls (Oxford, 1993)

Dobbins, Frank, '"Doulce Mémoire": A Study of the Parody Chanson', *PRMA* xcvi (1969–70), 85–102

Dodd, Gordon, 'A Study in Consort Interpretation: William Lawes, Six-part Consort Suite No. 2 in C', *Chelys,* v (1973–4) 42–50

—'William Lawes: Royall Consort Suite No. 9 in F', *Chelys,* vi (1975–6), 4–9

—*Thematic Index of Music for Viols,* i–vi (1980–92)

—'A Study in Consort Interpretation: William Lawes's Six-Part Consort Set in G minor', *Chelys,* xx (1991), 52–61

Doe, Paul, (ed.), *Elizabethan Consort Music II* (1988) = *MB* xlv

Dolmetsch, Mabel, *Dances of England and France from 1450 to 1600* (1949; R/New York, 1975)

—*Dances of Spain and Italy from 1400 to 1600* (1954)

Doughtie, Edward, *Lyrics from English Airs 1596–1622* (Cambridge, Mass., 1970)

Elizabethan Consort Music II, ed. Paul Doe (1988) = *MB* xlv

Erlebach, Rupert, 'William Lawes and his String Music', *PMA* lix (1932–3)

Evans, Willa McClung, *Henry Lawes, Musician and Friend of Poets* (New York, 1941)

Fane, Mildmay, *Otia Sacra* (1648; F/Delmar, New York, 1975)

[Fanshawe] *Notes, Genealogical and Historical, of the Fanshawe Family* (1868) no. 1

Fellowes, Edmund H., (ed.) *Eight Short Elizabethan Dance Tunes* (1924)

Ferrabosco, Alfonso, II, *Lessons for 1. 2. and 3. Viols* (1609; F/New York, 1973)

—*The Six-part Works,* ed. David Pinto (St Albans, 1990)

—*Four-part Fantasias for Viols,* ed. Andrew Ashbee and Bruce Bellingham (1992) = *MB* LXII

—*The Hexachord Fantasies in 5 and 4 parts,* ed. David Pinto (St Albans, 1992)

Field, Christopher, 'Matthew Locke and the Consort Suite', *M&L* li (1970) 15–25

Ford, Robert, 'Osborn MS 515: A Guardbook of Restoration Instrumental Music', *Fontes Artis Musicæ,* xxx (1983), 174–83

Gibbons, Orlando, *Six Fantasias for Viols in Six parts,* ed. Michael Hobbs (1982)

—*Consort Music,* ed. John Harper (1982) = *MB* XLVIII

Grant, Kerry S., *Dr Burney as Critic and Historian of Music* (Ann Arbor, 1983)

Gregg, Pauline, *King Charles I* (1981)

Hacket, John, *Scrinia Reserata* (1693)

Hamessley, Lydia, 'The Tenbury and Ellesmere Partbooks: New Findings on Manuscript Compilation and Exchange', *M&L* lxxiii (1992), 177–221

Hassler, Hans Leo, *Canzonette a Quatro Voci* (Nuremberg,1590)

Hawkins, Sir John, *A General History of the Science and Practice of Music* (1776; R/ 1853, R/intr. Charles Cudworth New York, 1963)

Hayes, Gerald, *King's Music* (1937)

Heath, Robert, *Clarastella* (1650)

Hingeston, John, *The Suites for Five & Six Viols,* ed. John Dornenburg (Albany, 1991)

—*The Fantasy-Suites for Four Viols,* ed. John Dornenburg (Albany, 1992)

Holman, Peter, 'The "Symphony"' *Chelys,* vi (1975–6), 10–24

—'New Sources of Music by Robert Johnson", *LSJ* xx (1978), 43–52

—'Thomas Baltzar (?1631–1663), The "Incomperable *Lubicer* on the Violin"', *Chelys,* xiii (1984) 3–38

—'The Harp in Stuart England: New Light upon William Lawes's Harp Consorts', *EM* xv (1987), 188–203

—*Four and Twenty Fiddlers* (Oxford, 1993)

Hudson, George, *Suite in G minor,* ed. Ila H. Stoltzfus (Ottowa, 1981)

Hudson, Richard, *The Folia, The Saraband, The Passacaglia, and the Chaconne i: The Folia* (Stuttgart, 1982)

Hulse, Lynn, 'John Hingeston', *Chelys,* xii (1983), 23–42

—'The Musical Patronage of Robert Cecil, First Earl of Salisbury (1563–1612)',
  JRMA cxvi (1991), 24–40
Hutchinson, Lucy, *Memoirs of [the Life of] Colonel Hutchinson,* ed. Julius Hutchinson
  (1908; R/1965)
Huxley, Gervase, *Endymion Porter 1587–1640* (1959)
Irving, John, 'Thomas Tomkins's Copy of Morley's "A Plain and Easy
  Introduction to Practical Music"', *M&L* lxxi (1990), 483–93
Jacobean Consort Music ed. William Coates and Thurston Dart (1955; 2/1962; 3/
  1971) = *MB* IX
Jenkins, John, *Consort Music of Four Parts,* ed. Andrew Ashbee (1969; 2/1975) =
  MB XXVI
—*Consort Music for Viols in Five Parts,* ed. Richard Nicholson (1971)
—*Consort Music for Viols in Six Parts,* ed. Richard Nicholson and Andrew Ashbee
  (1976)
—*Consort Music for Viols in Four Parts,* ed. Andrew Ashbee (1978)
—*Two Fantazia-Suites for Treble Viol (Violin) Bass Viol and Organ,* ed. Andrew Ashbee
  (Albany, 1991)
—*The Lyra Viol Consorts,* ed. Frank Traficante (Madison, 1992) = *RRMBE* LXVII–
  LXVIII
—*18 Four-Part Airs,* ed. Andrew Ashbee (St Albans, 1992)
—*Aires for Four-Part Consort,* ed. David Pinto (St Albans, 1992)
—*Seven Fancy-Ayre Division Suites for Two Trebles, Bass and Organ,* ed. Robert A.
  Warner, rev. Andrew Ashbee (2/1993)
—*Eight Aires,* ed. Andrew Ashbee (1993) = *SP* 167
Johnson, Robert, *Complete Works for Solo Lute,* ed. Albert Sunderman (Oxford,
  1972)
Jordan, Tho[mas], *The Muses Melody in a Consort of Poetrie* (n. d.)
King, A. Hyatt, *Some British Collectors of Music c.1600–1960* (Cambridge, 1963)
Klinkenborg, Verlyn, (ed.) with Herbert Cahoon, *British Literary Manuscripts Series*
  I: *from 800 to 1800* (New York, 1981)
Knyvett Letters, ed. Bertram Schofield (1949)
La Belle, Jenijoy, 'The Huntington Aston Manuscript', *The Book Collector,* xxix
  (1980), 542–67
Lawes, William, *Select Consort Music,* ed. Murray Lefkowitz (1963; 2/1971) = *MB*
  XXI
—*Pavan and Two Aires a4 in G minor,* ed. Layton Ring (1964)
—*Ayres a 3 voc:,* ed. Gordon Dodd (1966) = *SP* 38
—*Trois masques à la cour de Charles Ier d'Angleterre,* ed. Murray Lefkowitz (Paris,
  1970)
—*Consort Sets in Five and Six Parts,* ed. David Pinto (1979)
—*Suite no. 1 in C minor and Suite no.2 in C major for two treble and two bass viols,* ed.
  Richard Taruskin (Ottawa, 1983)
—*Fantasies and Aires 2 Trebles and 2 Basses to the Organ,* ed. Richard Nicholson
  (1985) = *ECS* xvii

185

Lawes, William, *Fantasia-Suites*, ed. David Pinto (1991) = *MB* LX

—*The Royall Consort, Old Version/New Version*, ed. David Pinto (1995)

Lawes, William and Henry, *Choice Psalmes* (1648)

Leech-Wilkinson, Daniel, 'The Thynne Lute Book', *The Lute = LSJ*, xxxiii (1993), 1–11

Lefkowitz, Murray, *William Lawes* (1960)

Leicester, Sir Peter, *Charges to the Grand Jury at Quarter Sessions 1660–1677*, ed. Elizabeth M. Halcrow (Manchester, 1953) = Chetham Society, Series 3, V

L'Estrange, Roger, *Truth and Loyalty Vindicated* (1667)

Locke, Matthew, *Chamber Music* i-ii, ed. Michael Tilmouth (1971–2) = *MB* XXXI–XXXII

Lindley, David, (ed.) *The Court Masque* (Manchester, 1984)

Lupo, Thomas, *The Four-Part Consort Music* ed. Richard Charteris and John M. Jennings (Clifden, 1983)

—*Two Madrigal-Fantasies* ed. David Pinto (Harpenden, 1990)

Louis XIII *Ballet du Roy 'La Merlaison'*, ed. Roger J. V. Cotte (Paris, 1992)

Mace, Thomas, *Musick's Monument* (Cambridge and London, 1676; F/Paris, 1966)

—Vol. ii: *Commentaire par Jean Jacquot Transcription par André Souris* (Paris, 1966)

Maniates, Maria Rika, *Mannerism in Italian Music and Culture, 1530–1630* (Manchester, 1979)

Marcus, Leah S., *The Politics of Mirth: Jonson, Herrick, Milton, Marvell, and the Defense of Old Holiday Pastimes* (Chicago, 1986)

Marenzio, Luca, *Madrigali a quatro cinque, et sei voci, Libro primo* (Venice, 1588)

Mersenne, Marin, *Harmonie Universelle* (Paris, 1636), F/intr. François Lesure (Paris, 1963)

Meyer, Ernst Hermann, 'Form in the Instrumental Music of the Seventeenth Century', *PMA* lxv (1938–9), 45–61

—*English Chamber Music* (1946; 2/1951) rev. as *Early English Chamber Music*, ed. E. H. Meyer and Diana Poulton (1982)

Mico, Richard, *The Complete Five-Part Works*, ed. Richard Nicholson (1977) = *ECS* ii

—*Consort Music*, ed. Andrew Hanley (1994) = *MB* LXV

Millar, Oliver, 'The Inventories and Valuation of the King's Goods 1649–1651', *Walpole Society* XLIII (1970–2)

Morgan, Irvonwy, *Prince Charles's Puritan Chaplain* (1957)

Music in Britain: The Seventeenth Century, ed. Ian Spink (Oxford, 1992) = *The Blackwell History of Music in Britain*, III

Nichols, John, *The Progresses ... of King James the First ...* (1828)

Norgate, Edward, *Miniatura or The Art of Limning*, ed. Martin Hardie (Oxford, 1919)

North, Dudley, *A Forest Promiscuous of Several Seasons Production* (2/1659)

North on Music, Roger , ed. John Wilson (1959)

Oman, Charles, *English Church Plate 597–1830* (Oxford, 1957)

Palme, Per, *Triumph of Peace: A Study of the Whitehall Banqueting House* (Uppsala, 1956)

Parker, G. and Smith, L. M., *The General Crisis of the Seventeenth Century* (1978)
Parry, Graham, *The Golden Age Restor'd: The Culture of the Stuart Court 1603–42* (Manchester, 1981)
Payne, Ian, (ed. and reconstr.) *Cambridge Consorts Pavans and Galliards in 5 parts* (St Albans, 1991)
Pickel, Margaret B., *Charles I as a Patron of Poetry and Drama* (1936)
Pinto, David, 'William Lawes' Music for Viol Consort', *EM* vi (1978), 12–24
—'The Fantasy Manner: The Seventeenth-Century Context', *Chelys*, x (1981), 17–28
—'William Lawes at the Siege of York, 1644', *MT* cxxvii (1986), 579–83
—'The Music of the Hattons' *RMA Research Chronicle*, xxiii (1990), 79–108
—'Music at Court: Remarks on the Performance of William Lawes's Works for Viols', Johannes Boer and Guido van Oorschot (eds.) *A Viola da Gamba Miscellany* (STIMU; Utrecht, 1994), 27–40
—'Gibbons in the Bedchamber', in A. Ashbee and P. Holman (eds.), *John Jenkins and his Time : Studies in English Consort Music,* (Oxford, forthcoming *a*)
—'New Lamps for Old: the Versions of the Royal Consort', (forthcoming *b*)
—'The True Christmas: Carols at the Court of Charles I', (forthcoming *c*)
—'Dowland's Tears: Aspects of *Lachrimæ*' (forthcoming *d*)
Playford, John, (ed.), *A Musicall Banquet* (1651*a*)
—*The English Dancing Master* (1651*b*) F/ed. Margaret Dean-Smith as *Playford's English Dancing Master* (1957)
—*Court-Ayres* (1655) = *CA*
—*Courtly Masquing Ayres* (1662) = *CMA*
—*The Musical Companion* (1673)
—*The Complete Country Dance Tunes from Playford's Dancing Master (1651–ca.1728)* ed. Jeremy Barlow (1985)
Poole, Rachael L., 'The Oxford Music School, and the Collection of Portraits Formerly preserved there' *MA* iv (1913), 143–159
Porter, Stephen, *Destruction in the English Civil Wars* (Stroud, 1994)
Poulton, Diana, *John Dowland* (1972; 2/1982)
Price, Curtis, *Music in the Restoration Theatre* (Ann Arbor, 1979)
—*Henry Purcell and the London Stage* (Cambridge, 1984)
Rastall, Richard, 'Benjamin Rogers (1614–98): Some Notes on His Instrumental Music' *M&L* xlvi (1965), 237–42
Ring, G. L., *A Preliminary Enquiry into the Continuo Parts of William Lawes for Organ, Harp and Theorbo'*, M.A. Thesis (Nottingham, 1972)
Robertson, Dora, *Sarum Close* (1938; R/Bath,1969)
Robinson, Thomas, *The Schoole of Musicke* (1603); F/transcr. and ed. David Lumsden (Paris, 1971)
Rogers, Malcolm, *William Dobson 1611–46* (catalogue of National Portrait Gallery exhibition, Oct. 1993–Jan. 1994) (1983)
Rostand, Ellen, 'The Descending Chromatic Tetrachord: An Emblem of Lament', *MQ* lxv (1979), 346–59
Sabol, Andrew J., *Four Hundred Songs and Dances from the Stuart Masque* (Providence, Rhode Island, 1978)

Sayce, Lynda, 'Performing Purcell: A Question Answered', *EMR* viii (Mar. 1995), 14–15

Scholes, Percy, *The Puritans and Music* (Oxford, 1934; R/1969)

Schuetze, George C., (ed.) *Settings of 'Ardo Sì' and its Related Texts* (Madison, 1990) = *RRMR* 78–9

Segerman, Ephraim, 'The Name "Tenor Violin"' *GSJ* xlviii (1995), 181–7

Sharpe, Kevin, *Criticism and Compliment* (Cambridge, 1987)

—*Politics and Ideas in Early Stuart England* (1989)

Sherwood, Roy, *The Court of Oliver Cromwell* (1977)

Shirley, E.P., *Stemmata Shirleiana* (1841; 2/1873)

Simpson, Christopher, *The Division-Viol* (2/1665; F/1965)

—*A Compendium of Practical Musick* (1667), ed. Phillip J. Lord (Oxford, 1970)

Simpson, Thomas, *Taffel-Consort (1621)*, ed. Bernard Thomas (1988)

Smuts, R. Malcolm, *Court Culture and the Origins of a Royalist Tradition in Early Stuart England* (Philadelphia, 1987)

Spink, Ian, *English Song Dowland to Purcell* (1974; 2/New York 1986)

—(ed.) *Music in Britain: The Seventeenth Century* (Oxford, 1992) = *The Blackwell History of Music in Britain*, III

Stone, Lawrence, *The Crisis of the Aristocracy 1558–1641* (Oxford,1965; 2/1966)

T[atham], I[ohn], *OSTELLA or the Faction of Love and Beauty reconcil'd* (1650)

Temperley, Nicholas, *The Music of the English Parish Church* (Cambridge, 1979)

Thompson, Robert, 'English Music Manuscripts and the Fine Paper Trade, 1648–1688' (PhD dissertation, University of London, 1988)

Tomkins, Thomas, *Consort Music*, ed. John Irving (1991) = *MB* LIX

Traficante, Frank, 'Music for the Lyra Viol: Manuscript Sources', *Chelys*, viii (1978–9), 4–22

Tyrell, S. J., *A Countryman's Tale* (1973)

Vaughan, Henry, *The Works of Henry Vaughan,* ed. L. C. Martin (2/Oxford, 1957)

—*The Complete Poems*, ed. Alan Rudrum (Harmondsworth, 1976)

Ward, John, *Madrigals and Elegies from Manuscript Sources*, ed. Ian Payne (1988) = *EMS* XXXVIII

—*Five In Nomines for Four Viols*, ed. Virginia Brookes (Albany, 1992)

—*Seven Fantasias*, ed. Virginia Brookes (Albany, 1993*a*)

—*Eight Fantasias*, ed. Virginia Brookes (Albany, 1993*b*)

—*Consort Music of Five and Six Parts*, ed. Ian Payne (1995) = *MB* lxvii

Ward, John M, *Sprightly & Cheerful Musick* = *LSJ* xxi (1979–81)

—'The English Measure', *EM* xiv (1986) 15–21

—'Newly Devis'd Measures for Jacobean Masques', *AM* x (1988), 111–42

Warlock, Peter, (ed.), *Six English Tunes...for String Quintet* (1926)

Wess, Joan, 'Musica Transalpina, Parody, and the Emerging Jacobean Viol Fantasia', *Chelys*, xv (1986), 3–25

Willetts, Pamela J., 'Sir Nicholas Le Strange and John Jenkins', *M&L* xlii (1961), 30–43

—*The Henry Lawes Manuscript* (1969)

—'Stephen Bing: A Forgotten Violist', *Chelys*, xviii (1989), 3–17

—'John Barnard's Collections of Viol and Vocal Music', *Chelys*, xx (1991), 28–42

Willetts, Pamela J., 'John Lilly: A Redating' *Chelys*, xxi (1992), 27–38

Wood, Anthony, *The Life and Times of Anthony Wood, Antiquary, of Oxford, 1632– 1695* ..., ed. Andrew Clark (Oxford, 1891–1900)

Woodfield, Ian, 'The First Earl of Sandwich, a Performance of William Lawes in Spain and the Origins of the Pardessus de Viole', *Chelys*, xiv (1985), 40–2

Woodfill, Walter L., *Musicians in English Society from Elizabeth to Charles I* (Princeton, New Jersey, 1953; R/New York, 1969)

Recordings

At the time of publication, the main collections discussed in this book are available on CD. The works for viols have been recorded by Fretwork on Virgin Veritas:

'Heart's Ease'	VC 7 59667
'For ye violls'	VC 7 59021
'Concord is conquer'd'	VC 5 45147.

The Royall Consort (New version) has been recorded by the Purcell Quartet on Chandos Chaconne:

'The Royall Consort Suites 1–10'   Chan 0584/0585.

Index